D1527942

ASTRONAUTS

NASA

ON

PARADE

ASTR🜨NAUTS
ON
PARADE

How NASA Public Affairs Brought American Astronauts to the World

GENE MARIANETTI

Acclaim Press™
MORLEY, MISSOURI

Acclaim Press
— Your Next Great Book —

P.O. Box 238
Morley, MO 63767
(573) 472-9800
www.acclaimpress.com

Editor: Randy Baumgardner
Book Design: Rodney Atchley
Cover Design: Frene Melton

ISBN: 978-1-948901-24-6 | 1-948901-24-2
Library of Congress Control Number: 2019901216

First Printing, 2019
Printed in the United States of America
10 9 8 7 6 5 4 3 2 1

This publication was produced using available information.
The publisher regrets it cannot assume responsibility for errors or omissions.

CONTENTS

FOREWORD

W ith words and seldom-seen historical pictures my colleague and good friend Gene Marianetti has captured the unique story of how NASA opened its missions and its people to the worldwide public. Shortly after NASA was established decisions made at the highest levels of government set up the American civilian space program to be shared with the people who would fund the effort, the American taxpayers. In doing so it meant the entire world would have access to the American effort in seeking President Kennedy's goal of "...landing a man on the Moon and returning him safely to the Earth."

This desired openness of NASA resulted in the formation of a somewhat unique public affairs organization with the job of telling all of the story, including successes *and* failures. Frankly, in the early days of NASA that openness was strikingly different for many of us...especially those of us who had prior experience with military programs. But, in short order we got used to being open, warts and all, and it became part of the DNA of NASA, which remains until this day.

After his arrival at NASA in 1967 Gene was responsible for the planning and proper execution of all major public events involving NASA, its officials and projects. This included public appearances by the Administrator, his senior staff, as well as national and worldwide appearances by astronauts. Gene also was responsible for the planning and coordination of agency-wide launch and landing guest operations at the Kennedy Space Center and Edwards Air Force Base.

The role of the Apollo-era astronauts in getting the NASA story across to the public was huge. As soon as they joined the astronaut corps, and well before they flew into space, the astronauts were recognized as national icons, which made them immediate "press darlings." After their missions into space, especially those who flew missions to the Moon, the astronauts' popularity soared even higher taking on the aura of rock stars! They were in extremely high demand to appear all over the world, and it was the mission of NASA's Public Affairs Office (PAO) to channel, plan, coordinate and control the astronaut's valuable time in dealing with domestic and worldwide leaders as well as public audiences...enter Gene Marianetti.

Gene's responsibilities over a 27-year career with NASA gave him a one-of-a kind inside view of a fascinating segment of American history in the making AND the people who made it happen. Gene experienced it all, and in *Astronauts on Parade* he shares that inside view in an easy-to-understand style. Oh, and he tells ALL of the story!

Gerry Griffin
Former Apollo Mission Control Flight Director
Former Director, Lyndon B. Johnson Space Center

Gerald D. (Gerry) Griffin is an aeronautical engineer who may be best be remembered as one of the flight directors in NASA's Mission Control who helped guide the crippled Apollo 13 spacecraft to a successful splashdown in 1970. He and his colleagues were honored for their efforts when awarded the Presidential Medal of Freedom by President Richard Nixon. He later served the agency in several senior administrative positions at NASA Headquarters in Washington, D.C. and retired after serving as the Director of the NASA Johnson Space Center in Houston, replacing space pioneer Christopher Columbus Kraft in 1982.

After the Apollo program was completed, Griffin transferred to NASA Headquarters where he was responsible for coordinating Congressional and public affairs liaison activities. He then served as deputy director of the Dryden (now Armstrong) Flight Research Center in California, and as deputy director of the Kennedy Space Center in Florida.

After taking early retirement from NASA in 1986, Gerry became a senior executive with several non-space, as well as space-related companies and organizations in the private sector. Today he remains active in several businesses and serves as a technical and management consultant for a broad range of clients.

He is a 1956 graduate of Texas A&M University, and served four years on active duty in the U.S. Air Force before joining NASA as a flight controller in Mission Control in 1964. He remains active as a general aviation pilot and aircraft owner and holds a commercial license. He has served as a technical adviser for the movie "Apollo 13" and other space movies and TV series. He and his wife Sandra (Sandy) have two children Kirk and Gwen and reside in Hunt, Texas. Griffin was born on Christmas Day in 1934 in Athens, Texas, and has a twin brother, Larry.

DEDICATION

The book is dedicated to many, and my sincere thanks to those who made it possible. While the astronauts rightfully deserve to be recognized for their roles, they will be the first to argue that Apollo and the space programs that followed were "team efforts." and the accomplishments belong to thousands.

I was fortunate to have played an important role helping the astronauts explain and market the space program here and abroad, especially after beginning the space race in a distant second place behind the USSR. The first Moon landing, which we celebrate this year fifty years later (2019), was the crowning achievement of the goal set by President Kennedy in 1961.

On a personal note, I am deeply indebted to my wife of 64 years, Peg, who was a stay-at home mom to our four kids while I traveled extensively in my job. I was gone almost six months in 1973, traveling three months with the Apollo 17 astronauts around the U.S. and a three-month trip to Africa and Asia supporting the crew on a Presidential Goodwill Tour.

And a special thank you to Ed Buckbee, an author and lecturer who began Space Camp in Huntsville, Alabama, for the advice and encouragement he provided in my decision to write this book.

Introduction

On July 20, 2019, NASA will celebrate the 50th Anniversary of Apollo 11, when America and the world watched Astronauts Neil Armstrong and Buzz Aldrin fulfill a challenge set in 1961 by President John F. Kennedy to land a man on the Moon and return him safely to Earth before the end of the decade.

It is still hailed as one of mankind's greatest engineering, scientific, and political achievements, and is often used in the context—"If we can land a man on the Moon, why can't we find a cure for cancer, end poverty, or solve other worthy but otherwise unobtainable causes?"

An estimated 400,000 Americans helped fulfill President Kennedy's national goal; however, at least two individuals, both with ties to North Carolina, should be recognized for the roles they played in achieving what seemed an unachievable challenge at the time.

James E. Webb, who had served as Director of the Budget under President Harry S Truman, reluctantly became NASA's second administrator, but only after some arm twisting by President Kennedy and Vice President Lyndon Johnson. Webb was originally a business executive who will be remembered for pulling together a Manhattan Project level team from many different fields including private industry, education, science, and government to meet the lunar landing challenge.

At the time, the U.S. was still trying to catch up with the Soviet Union and Sputnik, Yuri Gagarin—the first man in space—and a Cold War effort for world leadership in space technology and science.

Webb will be remembered as an extraordinary manager during his eight years at NASA, overcoming the tragic 1967 Apollo 1 fire, which took the lives of three astronauts, and his continued efforts to convince Congress of the need to appropriate the necessary funds to complete the goal set by President Kennedy. He realized that the space program would require a top notch public affairs effort to educate and inform the American people, and had been following the reporting of Julian Scheer, an author and reporter based in Charlotte, North Carolina.

It was Scheer's news coverage of space launches at Cape Canaveral that first caught Webb's attention. In fact, Webb was so impressed that he sought out Scheer to be his assistant administrator for public affairs. So, he called Scheer and asked him to write a plan that would shape the structure and policies into what could be a NASA Public Affairs team approach.

It took Scheer about a month to complete the plan and deliver it to Webb in Washington. A phone call followed, and he came to Washington to present his ideas. Scheer barely had time to be seated before Webb led with, "I accept your offer to go to work for me."

"I want you to run this program just as you've outlined it. You'll work directly for me," Webb said. "I will always support your public affairs decisions, but will fire you immediately if you're wrong."

The year was 1962. It was to become a perfect relationship.

ASTRONAUTS

ON

PARADE

How NASA Public Affairs Brought American Astronauts to the World

Chapter One

NASA PUBLIC AFFAIRS – THE EARLY YEARS

It was not without its ups and downs, but Webb trusted Scheer to make the right decisions and knew if there was a question he was always available to discuss it. Together, they built a public affairs organization that began at NASA Headquarters in Washington and was duplicated at the other fourteen NASA field centers.

Both realized the importance of creating a dynamic NASA public image that American taxpayers would come to accept and support. Public support for NASA was critical, but Webb and Scheer recognized the importance of transferring space-developed technology for use in the private sector, a process known as "Spinoff".

As a result, many of the items produced for space flight were made available for conversion to public use. A new branch, the Office of Technology Utilization, was established to monitor and transfer items to the private sector for development, marketing and sales.

Tang®, Teflon® and Velcro® were invented for consumers, not for the space program as was often claimed. State of the Art communication and weather satellites are obvious examples, but spinoff technologies have impacted consumer goods, heath, medicine, public safety, transportation, cyber space, energy and industrial productivity in the years since NASA was created.

The newsroom was central at NASA Headquarters, and on a smaller scale at each field center to serve the news media. At headquarters the newsroom was a bullpen arrangement, with a chief and small staff of public affairs officers (PAO's) to write and edit releases.

Scheer assigned other PAO's to each major program office, where they were co-located to work directly with associate or assistant administrators in the offices of aeronautics, space science, technology utilization, and international affairs in the development and preparation of news releases, publications and speeches.

Beginning with the acquisition of thousands of still pictures and reels of historical film from the National Advisory Committee (NACA), NASA's predecessor at Langley, Virginia, an audio/visual office was located near the newsroom at NASA Headquarters to support media requests and available to help PAO's.

A great many of the photographs and motion picture footage were taken by William (Bill) Taub, who began his photographic career at the age of seventeen at NACA before transferring to Washington when Congress created NASA in 1958.

Taub's photos have appeared in national publications including *National Geographic, Smithsonian, Time Magazine, Saturday Evening Post*, wire services, and NASA publications. He covered all of the manned space launches at Cape Canaveral and Kennedy Space Center, and was aboard the recovery ships at all the splashdowns.

He was the only photographer present at Cape Canaveral on January 27, 1967, when a flash fire swept through the Apollo 1 command module during a launch rehearsal test, claiming the lives of Astronauts Gus Grissom, Roger Chaffee and Ed White.

One of Webb's greatest contributions to the public affairs effort was his personal creation of the NASA Fine Arts Program. He felt well known artists could capture the excitement and meaning of space flight to commemorate future historic events of the American space program.

At his direction, the effort was started by James Dean, NASA's art and graphics director. Working with J. Carter Brown, Director of the National Art Gallery, they created the NASA Fine Arts Program, approaching famous artists like Bob McCall, who painted the huge murals in the lobby of the National Air and Space Museum.

A team of artists was assigned to every major space event. They were paid a small stipend to cover travel and lodging expenses, and in return each donated a piece of their finished art for consideration by NASA and inclusion in the permanent program inventory.

A coffee table book "Eyewitness to Space" features 258 paintings, drawings and prints by forty-seven of some of the most renowned artists including Paul Calle, George Weymouth, Robert Rauschenberg, and McCall. Many of their works are on display at art galleries and museums around the country.

Even before the advent of VCR's and the digital age, NASA produced a weekly series of five minute radio and filmed TV programs named *NASA's Space and Aeronautics Report* for distribution to stations for airing as a public service.

Space Mobile, a national space mobile demonstration program, was developed for NASA by noted author James Bernardo and operated under contract originally by Chico State University in California.

Mobile vans were purchased and equipped with models and other space related exhibits and operated by retired school teachers or individuals with science backgrounds familiar with NASA programs. They would travel the country and conduct workshops at selected schools.

Scheer organized a Special Events Division with branch chiefs to support the Administrator in speech preparation and travel, an office for scheduling astronauts and speakers, and a branch for planning, organizing and manning a guest operation at the Kennedy Space Center for the Apollo launches, as well as a liaison office for coordination with Congress and the White House.

Webb and Scheer held many discussions about ways to maintain public interest and support of the space program while NASA was working to implement recommended changes to the Apollo spacecraft after the flash fire. Both agreed on the importance of getting the astronauts out of their flight suits and into the public consciousness before the return to space.

Chapter Two

TURNING ASTRONAUTS INTO AMBASSADORS FOR SPACE FLIGHT

S cheer and Alan Shepard, chief of the astronaut office, discussed ways to develop a plan where available astronauts would make appearances to better educate the public about NASA and the Apollo program. The discussions resulted in an agreement called a NASA Management Issuance (NMI). It outlined three categories of appearances: 1) Technical, 2) HQ, and 3) Management.

The astronaut office would be responsible for those of a technical nature, while all Headquarters requests would be scheduled on behalf of the Administrator. Not always, but occasionally, one of these requests would be flagged as "Must Do" if it involved senior NASA management, member of Congress, the White House or State Department.

There were times when such requests required additional information or justification because of possible fund raising implications or an event considered inappropriate for astronaut participation. Upon completion of a space flight, debriefings and a press conference, the returning astronauts were available for three months of public appearance scheduling known as Post Flight.

During Post Flight, the astronauts were scheduled as a crew and made individual appearances. Many were personal and included hometown returns, visits to their colleges, universities, military academies, major cities, and the like.

Trips to Washington almost always included visits to the White House, appearances before key congressional committees and meeting individually with important U.S. Senators and Congressmen. Six times in the first years of the Space Age, NASA astronauts addressed joint meetings of the U.S. Senate and House of Representatives. The first was by John Glenn, on February 26, 1962, just days after his historic *Friendship 7* flight.

Gordon Cooper, who flew *Faith 7*, the last flight in the Mercury program, spoke to a joint meeting on May 21, 1963, and he and fellow Astronaut Pete Conrad spoke at a joint meeting following their Gemini 5 mission on September 15, 1965.

The Apollo 8 crew with Frank Borman, Bill Anders and Jim Lovell were introduced and addressed a joint meeting of the Congress on January 9, 1969. They were followed by the first lunar landing crew, Apollo 11, at a joint meeting on September 16, 1969.

The Apollo 17 crew, commanded by Gene Cernan and including Ron Evans and Harrison Jack Schmitt, participated in the second inauguration of President Nixon, and spoke at a session of the U.S. House of Representatives two days later on January 22, 1973.

Since 1968, an estimated eighty-five books have been written by or about astronauts, with little reference about the important role they played both before, and after, their spaceflights. It was public relations and their ability to share with the press and public the personal experience of flying in space and to the Moon and gaining the edge over the Soviet Union in the space race that helped fuel NASA during the Apollo and Space Shuttle years.

With the selection of the Original 7 in 1959, astronauts were chosen because of their proven capabilities and the ability to fly high performance aircraft, not because of their public personae or presentation skills. The media would assume that responsibility with the help of the NASA Public Affairs Office through newsletters, press kits, releases, press conferences, interviews and many hundreds of personal public appearances.

President Kennedy's bold 1961 challenge to land a man on the Moon and return him safely to Earth before the end of the decade was in serious jeopardy after the Apollo 1 fire. This courageous challenge by a young president on May 25, 1961, was less than three weeks after Alan Shepard's sub-orbital flight and still about nine months before John Glenn's *Friendship 7* flight, when he would become the first American in space on February 20, 1962.

Between December of 1968 and December of 1972, twenty-four American astronauts flew to the Moon; twelve landed and walked on the lunar surface, three (Jim Lovell, Gene Cernan, and John Young) flew to the Moon twice, and none of them landed more than once.

At this writing, only four Moonwalkers are still living: Buzz Aldrin (Apollo 11), David Scott (Apollo 15), Charlie Duke (Apollo 16) and Harrison Jack Schmitt (Apollo 17). Apollo 12 astronaut Alan Bean, the fourth man to walk on the Moon, died unexpectedly in Houston on May 26, 2018.

Glenn was the first Astronaut to make a foreign trip in 1962. Since then astronauts have traveled to hundreds of countries, many on behalf of the sitting U.S President, to every state in the union and U.S. territories, including Puerto Rico, Guam and Saipan.

The purpose of this book is to share with readers my personal firsthand experiences, especially during the Apollo era. Accounts include many photographs, letters and other memorabilia as we approach the 50th anniversary of the first lunar landing on July 20, 1969. There will be many books written during the anniversary year by surviving astronauts and writers who have long and distinguished careers covering NASA and the space program.

While I have a journalism background, most of my experience before entering U.S. Government service was in broadcasting followed by a congressional internship. I am the first to acknowledge that I am not an author, but with the help of others, primarily Acclaim Press editors, I believe I have a story to tell and am now able to provide a documented account of what we were able to accomplish in space and the people and events that made it possible. This book will be of interest to those living during the beginning of the Space Age, and those who learned about it in books, movies, and television.

During the Space Age, astronauts made hundreds of radio and TV interviews, including the *Today Show*, *Good Morning America*, *Tonight Show* and other programs, thank you visits to NASA contractor facilities, and the agency's field centers to thank and acknowledge the contributions of their employees leading to the success of the Apollo program.

These visits were a vital function in meeting the requirements of the Space Act of 1958, which called "for the widest practicable and appropriate dissemination of information to the media and general public concerning NASA activities and results." Astronaut appearances played a vital role in the agency's efforts to comply with this directive.

This concludes the prelude and the beginning of a book I hope provides readers with the opportunity to identify with NASA and the lasting legacy the astronauts created, particularly the important role their public appearances played in the total context of a better public understanding of the space program.

Chapter Three

WEEK IN THE BARREL

M y arrival at NASA Headquarters in Washington, in August 1967, coincided with the selection of eleven scientist astronauts; three were physicians, three astronomers, two physicists, two engineers and one chemist. They joined the six scientist astronauts selected in 1965 and the nineteen chosen in 1966.

It brought the Astronaut Corps to about sixty-three individuals, which included Alan Shepard, Deke Slayton, Wally Schirra and Gordon Cooper from the Original 7. Slayton and Shepard were restricted from space flight assignments because of health-related issues, but accepted important administrative positions.

Slayton was director of Flight Crew Operations and Shepard, Chief of the Astronaut Office. It was about this time that both John Glenn and Scott Carpenter left NASA. Glenn returned to Ohio to campaign for election to the U.S. Senate, and Carpenter returned to the U.S Navy to head its Deep Submergence Program.

The addition of nine astronauts in 1962 and fourteen in 1963, followed by twenty-five in 1965 and 1966, and nineteen in 1966 brought the astronaut corps to the anticipated number needed for Apollo flight crew assignments.

Slayton was quick to announce his displeasure when the latest eleven arrived at the Manned Spacecraft Center in 1967, saying "that they had been hired because the government forced NASA to," and did not expect any of them to fly because of the surplus of astronauts. But he offered to accept their resignations and promised ground assignments if they chose to stay." Jokingly, the men named themselves "the XS-11" or Excess Eleven.

Seven members of the group who stayed with the program went on to form the core of early Space Shuttle Mission Specialists involving a total of fifteen flights. One in that group, Dr. Story Musgrave, a physician, had served in the U.S. Marines and developed a flying passion, logging over 17,700 hours in 160 different types of military and civilian aircraft, and flew six Space Shuttle flights before retiring in 1997.

But many selected by NASA a year earlier in 1966, which John Young labeled the "Original 19" in parody of the Original 7, would go on to play vital roles in the development of the Apollo command and service modules and the lunar landing module, eventually earning space flight assignments.

Nine from this group of nineteen flew in the Apollo program (Fred Haise and Jack Swigert, Apollo 13), (Stuart Roosa and Ed Mitchell, Apollo 14) (Jim Irwin and Al Worden, Apollo 15) (Charlie Duke and Ken Mattingly, Apollo 16) and (Ron Evans, Apollo 17).

While Slayton had grudgingly accepted the eleven new astronauts, they were a bonus for public affairs in seeking to fill a backlog of speaking requests since the completion of the Gemini program and the tragic loss of the Apollo 1 crew.

NASA was busy planning for the second Apollo lunar landing mission (Apollo 12), scheduled in November, when the U.S. Air Force announced the cancellation of the Manned Orbiting Laboratory (MOL) program which began in 1963 using a converted Gemini spacecraft for a top secret military mission manned space program to spy on the Soviet Union.

Seven military pilots from that program were accepted by NASA on August 14, 1969 and joined the astronaut corps in Houston. All would eventually fly aboard Space Shuttle flights.

The seven who all made Space Shuttle flights were Karol (Bo) Bobko, Robert L. Crippen, Gordon Fullerton, Henry Hartsfield, Robert Overmyer, Donald Peterson and Richard Truly, who flew two shuttle missions including commander of the first night launch STS-8 and would later serve as Administrator of NASA. He, Crippen and Bobko survive at this writing. Overmyer died in 1996, Fullerton in 2013, Hartsfield 2014 and Peterson in 2018.

Crippen was Commander John Young's pilot when the two flew the Space Shuttle *Columbia*'s first space flight in April 1981 and commanded three additional flights before eventually serving as director of the John F. Kennedy Space Center.

Another member of the MOL group who would have probably transferred to NASA, and may have become the first NASA African American astronaut, was Air Force Major Robert H. Lawrence, who was killed at age 32 in the crash of his F-104 jet at Edwards Air Force Base in 1967.

The circumstances surrounding his death remained unknown for years because of the secrecy of the MOL Program. But his wife Barbara, who died in 2016, mounted a campaign that eventually broke a bureaucratic barrier over the" definition of astronaut", and he was finally recognized on the 50th anniversary of his death when his name was added to the Astronauts Memorial Foundation's Space Mirror at the Kennedy Space Center Complex, which honors astronauts who made the ultimate sacrifice.

Following approval of the astronaut NMI agreement, Shepard circulated a memorandum dictating that any astronaut not assigned to a space flight, backup, support crew or otherwise off- limits, was expected to make at least one public appearance a month, and he instituted a unique "Week in the Barrel" program primarily for the most recently selected astronauts.

It's believed that Shepard borrowed the name "Week in the Barrel" from a popular Navy joke. To say someone is in the "barrel" or taking a turn in the barrel means it's their turn to an unpleasant task or suffer an unpleasant experience.

The names of available "barrel" astronauts were furnished months in advance by the Astronaut Office for one week of scheduling by my office during a month. Every attempt was made to schedule as many as three stops on a trip with the first on a Monday, travel on Tuesday, appearances on Wednesday, travel on Thursday and a final schedule on Friday, enabling the astronaut to be home for the weekend.

When possible, astronauts used a T-38 supersonic jet trainer to fly to and from the appearances, which helped them maintain required flight efficiency but was a good public relations tool. It was an impressive site for event sponsors watching the astronaut's arrival.

In staffing most of the Week in the Barrel appearances, it was my job to help each individual develop an effective presentation with emphasis on tailoring style, manner and text depending on the nature of the audiences. Each appearance was evaluated and critiqued with suggestions and guidance in developing speech habits and tips for future presentations. Jack Swigert was my first "Barrel" participant.

I quickly learned that he had no experience as a public speaker the night before a scheduled breakfast speech before a group in Williamsburg, Virginia. He had written the speech and practiced his delivery in front of his hotel room mirror the night before. Eventually, he learned to prepare remarks on three by five cards and by the time he flew on Apollo 13 he had vastly improved his speaking ability.

Some of the astronauts were naturally gifted and able to deliver prepared remarks and remained at ease at the podium, but most were military pilots with little or no experience at public speaking and had to learn as they went along.

In between managing astronaut appearances, I began working with the director of our Special Events Division, Wade St. Clair, in preparing an agency-wide guest operations plan for the invitation and accommodation of guests for the upcoming Apollo launches beginning in 1968 at the Kennedy Space Center. The idea began with Webb and was Scheer's responsibility to create.

St. Clair and I were joined in this effort by Jim Funkhouser, who would become St. Clair's deputy and would figure prominently in the planning and management of all major NASA events including launches and appearances by the returning Apollo astronauts between 1969 and 1973.

He had begun his career at the Marshall Space Flight Center in Huntsville, Alabama, but became the public affairs representative at the Marshall facility located at Michoud, near New Orleans, before joining us in Washington.

St. Clair was a man of many talents as I learned during our brief five years working together. Scheer had become familiar with his work in the Charlotte broadcast media and wanted him at NASA to produce NASA's Space and Aeronautics report, a five minute taped public services program produced for local radio and TV stations across the country.

The show needed a narrator, and St. Clair auditioned several local announcers before hiring Willard Scott, a popular local radio announcer. Upon selecting Scott, who later rose to prominence as the weatherman on NBC's *Today Show*, St. Clair learned that he had been appearing and voicing commercials for McDonald's.

When told of Scott's selection, Scheer reportedly said, "Great, I've got to tell the administrator that we just hired Ronald McDonald as the voice of NASA." Scott continued in that role for years until he asked to be replaced, citing the demands of the *Today Show*. Ironically, Scott delivered the eulogy at St. Clair's funeral service in 2003, and was honored by NASA with a public service award.

The Guest Operation Plan was perhaps the first time a U.S. government agency developed and planned in advance a program to invite and accommodate thousands of guests and the general public to watch each of the upcoming Apollo launches from the John F. Kennedy Space Center.

It was Webb's desire for both invited guests and the general public to watch and participate in a program they were paying for with tax dollars. At the same time, it was a cooperative effort involving NASA Headquarters and all fourteen NASA field centers sharing equally in a launch invitation process.

During Mercury and Gemini, guest activities were individual efforts operated by the public affairs offices at the Kennedy, Marshall and Houston space centers. They were parochial, highly competitive and viewed as lost opportunities to tell the NASA story in the most impressive way possible.

The final plan was presented by Scheer at a briefing for Webb and representatives from all program and staff offices. It began with "Beginning with Apollo 4, an agency-wide program for handling all NASA guests will be in effect." A guest center staffed by public affairs protocol officers from the three centers with overall coordination by Headquarters would open at Cocoa Beach several days prior to the scheduled launch date.

The invitation process actually began weeks before a scheduled launch when all headquarters offices, field centers, and the astronaut office were invited to submit names of nominees to receive launch invitations.

Nominees from the NASA field centers included state and local elected officials, educators, business leaders, contractors and individuals representing a broad cross section of each NASA center. Included in their nominations were workers and contractors cited for their work in the Manned Flight Awareness (MFA) program. All invitations were extended by the Administrator.

With the exception of NASA-furnished bus transportation, guests participated at their own expense, and the invitation included an opportunity to tour the Kennedy Space Center and Cape Canaveral and receive a briefing by an individual familiar with the mission. Participation by an astronaut who was familiar with the mission greatly enhanced the presentation.

Our first opportunity to test the guest operation was the unmanned launch of the massive Saturn V launch vehicle on November 9, 1967. Atop the giant rocket was the Apollo 4 spacecraft, similar to the one that would be used for all the Apollo Moon flights.

Two unmanned launch tests remained before NASA could be confident that most of the needed hardware to begin the manned Apollo program was in place. Apollo 5 was successfully launched aboard a Saturn IB rocket, which would be used on the first manned Apollo 7 mission.

While confident after the success of the first Saturn V rocket on Apollo 4, NASA decided on one final Saturn V rocket launch to be sure everything was in place for the beginning of the Apollo program. While Apollo 6 experienced a few minor anomalies during its brief flight, NASA certified the vehicle ready for manned lunar missions.

The majority of people at launches had obtained free car passes, which were distributed on a first-come basis by Headquarters and field centers. This process allowed families to enter KSC and the Air Force Cape Canaveral Air Force Station and park on wide road shoulders in view of the launch pad and listen to countdown commentary from Launch Control. The car passes also encouraged families to visit the KSC Visitors Center and purchase inexpensive tickets for a guided bus tour of KSC and Cape Canaveral.

The guest center for each launch would open (usually in a banquet room of a local Cocoa Beach motel) five days prior to a scheduled launch date and was staffed by a NASA headquarters representative (usually me) and representatives from the Kennedy, Marshall and Manned Spacecraft Centers. Cocoa Beach was the center of activity because of its access to our resources at the Kennedy Space Center, buses, manpower, and support services.

The Apollo 4 launch on November 9, 1967, was a learning experience for me, dealing with non-public affairs individuals who were there to assist the special guests of their center director. I recall having breakfast with Ed Riddick and Vivian Whitley, who were there to look after personal guests of Dr. Wernher von Braun, Director of the Marshall Space Flight Center (MSFC), Alabama.

He and his team of rocket experts surrendered to the U.S. forces following the collapse of Germany in World War II, and were brought here where they pioneered our early rockets in New Mexico and then moved to Redstone Arsenal in Huntsville, where they developed the Saturn family of rockets including the mighty Saturn V used on every Apollo lunar mission.

We had a nice chat, and when it came time to order I asked Ed about grits and when he learned that I had never tried them, he instructed the waiter to bring a large order. When the bowl arrived steaming hot, I smiled and said, "Looks like cream of wheat to me, do I just add sugar and milk," and Ed, breaking out in a laughing smile, replied, "Only if you're a Yankee, just add butter, salt and pepper, and if available, red eye gravy."

Ed and Vivian worked for Bart Slattery, Director of Public Affairs for MSFC. Bart and I had adjoining rooms at the Holiday Inn, and during the course of our stay we discovered a mutual love of gin martinis, so I accepted his invitation to come to his room where he mixed a Gordon's gin martini.

It was on the rocks and when I mentioned that the drink lacked a touch of vermouth, he smiled took the drink from my hand and whispered "vermouth", explaining he only mixed them very dry. I couldn't bring myself to ask about an olive or twist of lemon, and we enjoyed a second martini before leaving for dinner.

Briefings and tours were scheduled in the morning and early afternoon and each bus was staffed by a volunteer representative from one of the Kennedy Space Center programs offices who conducted the tour and provided information about the launch guests were about to see.

On launch day, the same buses would congregate in the parking lot of the motel, and guests would board for transportation to the launch viewing site. Following liftoff and confirmation that the spacecraft had reached successful orbit, the buses would return guests to Cocoa Beach.

The majority of invited guests were handled in this manner, but each launch provided an opportunity for Webb and succeeding administrators to authorize the use of NASA administrative aircraft and on occasion a charter plane from Special Air Missions at Andrews Air Force Base.

The U.S. Air Force maintained a fleet of planes there, including the President's Air Force One. Most of the planes were KC 135's, which were converted from re-fueling to passenger configurations. Special invitation letters from the administrator were extended to members of

Congress, particularly those on key committees, representatives from the Defense Department and from agencies important to NASA, i.e. Energy, FAA, Smithsonian and Cabinet offices.

Because of its unique mission, NASA had received permission to acquire and use four 12-seat Grumman Gulfstream I turbo prop planes to transport astronauts, officials and space contractor personnel. NASA 1 was based at the Langley Research Center in Virginia, and was available to fly the administrator and other Washington officials. NASA 2 was assigned to the Manned Spacecraft Center in Houston, NASA 3 to Marshall Space Flight Center in Huntsville, Alabama and NASA 4 was based at Patrick Air Force Base in Cocoa Beach.

The planes were of great use in scheduling astronaut appearances during and after the Apollo program. Without the availability of these planes, it would have been difficult, if not impossible, to schedule the returning astronauts, their spouses and a small support staff to events around the country relying on commercial flights.

It was about the time that the Apollo program was getting started that the country was learning to cope with a series of 1968 tragic events, beginning with the attack and capture of the USS *Pueblo* by North Korea in January, the assassinations of the Reverend Martin Luther King Jr. in April, Senator Robert F. Kennedy in June, and the increased military involvement of the U.S. in Vietnam leading to riots and demonstrations in cities and on college campuses, and the raucous demonstrations at the National Democratic Convention in Chicago.

NASA had spent 20 months fixing problems with the command module, which had been revealed as the cause of the fire that killed the Apollo 1 crew, and with much of the hardware successfully tested, was ready for Apollo 7, an engineering test flight of the command and service modules. It would be the first time for a three-person American space crew launched aboard a Saturn IB rocket.

Wally Schirra, one of the Original 7 astronauts, who flew in Mercury and Gemini, was the commander with fellow astronauts Donn Eisele and Walter Cunningham making their first and what would be their last space flights. Apollo 7 was launched on October 11, 1968 and spent ten days and twenty hours in orbit, and completing every detailed test objective including the first live television broadcast from a manned spacecraft.

Chapter Four

THE RETIREMENT OF JAMES WEBB

B ecause of the frequency of the launches—projected to be one every two or three months—long range planning was involved. With the October 22, 1968 splashdown of Apollo 7 and certification of the command and service modules, development of the lunar module (LM) was behind schedule and NASA was forced to make a bold decision even before the next launch.

Management was faced with putting the Apollo program on hold, which it could ill afford. George Low, head of the spacecraft program office in Houston, presented a bold, but daring, solution. It called for launching the Apollo 8 command and service modules to the Moon without the LM.

The plan raised many eyebrows but after considerable discussion, it was determined that the announcement would be withheld until the Apollo 7 command/service modules could be certified after the flight.

Once it became known that Apollo 8 would be the first manned launch to the Moon, interest soared and we were inundated with requests to see Frank Borman, Jim Lovell and Bill Anders become the first humans to escape the bonds of Earth and fly to the Moon.

St. Clair and I arrived at the Kennedy Space Center five days before the launch to help our public affairs personnel who were already making final arrangements for our guest center, located in the banquet room of the Quality Inn on North Atlantic Avenue in Cocoa Beach.

Desks had been arranged for St. Clair and me and for representatives from the three manned spacecraft centers. Guests were welcomed, provided with Apollo 8 mission invitation packets, attended briefings, and boarded buses for tours of the Kennedy Space Center and the Air Force facilities at Cape Canaveral.

The previous three unmanned launches and the first manned Apollo 7 had drawn about 20,000 guests, and we estimated that more than twice that number would watch the Apollo 8 liftoff from a special viewing site three and a half miles from the launch pad.

An additional quarter of a million people lined the roads to the Kennedy Space Center as the giant Saturn V rocket roared to life and slowly lifted in a sea of flame engulfing Launch Pad 39-A at 7:51 a.m. on December 21. The historic mission lasted just over six days with the splashdown and recovery by the USS *Yorktown* in the North Pacific Ocean on December 27.

The flight lifted the country's spirits after what many considered one of the darkest times in our history. It also gave us the first look at the Earth from the Moon and Bill Anders photo of the famous Earthrise photo. Anders was quoted after the flight that he had gone to explore the Moon but ended up discovering the Earth.

The crew will forever be remembered for orbiting the Moon on Christmas Eve and reciting quotes from the "Book of Genesis", and for the record number of worldwide media and the thousands of guests who watched the launch and for the millions who watched on television.

One of the many guests flown by NASA to the launch was Senator George Murphy, the Republican Senator from California and former movie star. A staunch Catholic, he expressed interest in attending Mass prior to the launch. As a Catholic myself, I volunteered to accompany the Senator, and we attended a special Mass at The Church of Our Savior in Cocoa Beach.

The night before the launch, Scheer had organized an informal cocktail party for a select group of guests. While I can't remember the names of all those attending, I do remember Charles Lindbergh and Walter Cronkite being there.

Just prior to the Apollo 7 launch, Webb announced his retirement and made plans to attend what would be his first launch since being appointed Administrator by President Kennedy in 1961.

He always felt that his job was to remain in Washington, and fully trusted those on the launch team in Florida to make the right decisions. This was to be a going away present for the man whose leadership is credited with winning the race to put a man on the Moon. While many were responsible for the unfortunate launch pad accident, Webb himself accepted the blame so that the program could continue.

A lifelong Democrat from North Carolina, he left government service and returned to the private sector in 1953. Webb's name resurfaced in 1960 when JFK and LBJ were searching for a NASA Administrator. Webb had to be convinced that he was the right person for the job, expressing his feeling it should be someone with experience in rocketry. It was only after JFK convinced him that the job would be related to policy rather than rocketry that he accepted.

With the help of Hugh Dryden, who had been Deputy NASA Administrator, and the addition of MIT professor Dr. Robert C. Seamans Jr. as the Associate Administrator, they began the task of assembling perhaps one of the greatest management teams in history, involving industry, education, science, engineering and government.

Webb's experience in dealing with Congress would prove critical in obtaining the funds NASA would need to achieve the goal of President Kennedy. During his tenure there were more than 35,000 NASA civil service employees who were supported by more than 400,000 contractors employed in all fifty states.

Congressional budget hearings became extremely contentious after the Apollo 1 accident and the NASA management team found it increasingly difficult to obtain the necessary funds required to support the Apollo program and hopefully meet the goal set by President Kennedy.

Webb was a longtime Washington insider, and his experience as the budget director and Undersecretary of State during the Truman Administration made him a master at bureaucratic politics, which he successfully used to increase NASA's budget from $500 million in 1960 to a high point of $5.2 billion in 1965.

He was also known for his feisty reputation, and he often sparred with Senator William Proxmire of Wisconsin over NASA's funding. He was a constant critic of what he felt was wasteful government spending and led the effort that eventually resulted in the cancellation of a contract with the Boeing Company to build a U.S. supersonic airliner (SST) to compete with the British/French Concorde and Soviet SST's.

One story worth recalling occurred during a Senate hearing when Proxmire lectured Webb about being another government bureaucrat who was "chauffeured around in one of those big fancy limousines." Webb was quick to respond and invited the Senator to see the car during the luncheon break.

Proxmire would have been surprised to learn that Webb, while able to select the use of any vehicle from the General Services motor pool, had selected an economic Checker, famous as a taxicab in New York City.

I have the greatest admiration for his decision to retire just before he would bask in the glory of Apollo 11, which was just months away. He always felt that it was his responsibility to complete all the necessary preparations, and then let the others complete the journey.

It was viewed as an unselfish act, which proved that he really cared more for the success of the mission than the glory that would follow it. That honor would go to his eventual replacement, Deputy Administrator Dr. T.O. Paine.

Years later the Smithsonian acknowledged his work with establishment of the James E. Webb Internship for minority undergraduate juniors and graduate students in business and public administration to promote excellence in the management of not-for-profit organizations.

NASA Headquarters named its auditorium in his honor, and a space telescope developed in coordination with the European and Canadian space agencies and bearing his name will be launched in 2020 to replace the Hubble Space Telescope.

While best remembered for his role in leading to the Moon landings, Webb was responsible for NASA's space science programs, the unmanned missions to Venus and Mars and the development of weather and communications satellites.

In 1969, he was presented with the Presidential Medal of Freedom, having received the NASA Distinguished Service Medal in 1968 and the Langley Gold Medal from the Smithsonian Institution in 1976.

Chapter Five

TICKER TAPE FOR APOLLO 8

Immediately after the Apollo 8 launch, we began to respond to the thousands of requests for appearances by the crew. It was late December, and we were caught dealing with the outgoing Lyndon B. Johnson administration and the incoming Richard Nixon's transition team. Following the necessary debriefings in Houston, the astronauts and their wives were flown to Washington.

At the White House on January 8, President Johnson presented the NASA Distinguished Service Medal to the three astronauts saying, "Gentlemen, I am very proud to be privileged to present you with the NASA Distinguished Service Medals. They are very small tokens of our appreciation for what you have done for our country and for the world and for us.

"This is the last time I shall participate in a space ceremony as President of the United States. I am proud I have stood with the space effort from its first days and I am so glad to see it now flower in this most marvelous achievement."

The crew then responded and presented him with a plaque displaying the American flag and Apollo 8 mission patch hey had flown on their historic mission.

During the ceremony, the President introduced Webb and credited him with being most responsible for the success of the Apollo program and that he was the best administrator in the government.

The following day on January 9, Borman and his fellow crewmen addressed a joint meeting of Congress describing the experience of being the first humans to break the bonds of Earth and fly some 240,000 miles to orbit the Moon. Following lunch with the House and Senate Leadership, the astronauts spent the rest of the day signing autographs and making individual presentations to key members of the space committees.

I recall Jim Lovell telling me they had a good visit with former President Eisenhower, who was hospitalized at Walter Reed. They thanked him for his efforts in creating NASA and for his support of the space program. He died later that year, never able to leave the hospital.

In discussions with the three astronauts, we began to develop a plan that would include their participation in the upcoming Richard M. Nixon Presidential Inaugural January 19-20. Frank and Susan Borman and Jim and Marilyn Lovell agreed, but Bill and Valarie Anders could not attend because of a previous planned vacation in Mexico.

Schirra, who had already announced his intention to leave NASA and retire from the Navy, agreed to attend the Inauguration along with his fellow crewmates. It was not long after he retired that he joined CBS commentator Walter Cronkite and helped provide expert commentary for the remaining Apollo missions. He and Cronkite will be remembered for their emotional reactions describing the Apollo 11 landing on July 20.

After addressing Congress, the astronauts were flown to New York for a ticker tape parade down Broadway, similar to the ones for Charles Lindbergh, General Douglas MacArthur, Alan Shepard and John Glenn.

They were then honored in ceremonies at City Hall, and Governor Nelson Rockefeller hosted a luncheon at the Lincoln Center where each received Gold Medals. This was followed by a visit to the United Nations and a presentation before Secretary General U Thant and delegates from 123 nations. The New York visit concluded that night with a state dinner at the Waldorf Astoria, hosted by Governor Rockefeller.

Next on the schedule was a flight from New York to Miami, where they had been invited by NFL Commissioner Pete Rozelle to participate in the third NFL-AFL championship game between the Baltimore Colts and the New York Jets. It was the first game to officially bear the trademark "Super Bowl."

On game day, January 12, the crew was introduced at midfield and recited the "Pledge of Allegiance" before the playing of the National Anthem. It was an exciting game won by the underdog Jets 16-7. Their quarterback, the flamboyant Joe Namath, had guaranteed the win.

The following morning the crew boarded a NASA plane to Chicago for another ticker tape parade and a luncheon hosted by Mayor Richard Daley, who honored the crew with City of Chicago Gold Medals.

I was assigned to work with veteran NASA public affairs officer Ed Pierce to help with the crew's Chicago visit. Pierce had worked previous Mercury and Gemini crew visits, and on arrival I quickly learned his was a difficult assignment, dealing with Mayor Daley's staff and in particular his director of special events Jack (Black Jack) Reilly.

Perhaps it was the menacing black patch over his left eye that earned him the Black Jack moniker, but just his mention got the attention of police and other staff members. His demands were always in the name of Mayor Daley, but Pierce held his ground and won almost every argument.

With a schedule in place we were ready for the crew's arrival. Pierce said it would be best for me to accompany NASA's security representative Arnold Garrett in the motorcade. It was a new experience for me, and I just followed Garrett alongside the car carrying the astronauts.

Supporting Pierce in Chicago was a learning experience for me and demonstrated the importance of preliminary planning for astronaut trips, developing detailed schedules, arranging airport arrivals, motorcades, seating assignments, press conferences, dinners, luncheons, and coordination with law enforcement, security crowd control and finding opportunities for astronaut wives who accompanied their husbands on many of the trips. A top priority was the movement of astronauts and wives to and from events and the handling of autograph requests, exchange of gifts and presentation items, and thank you letters.

It was about this time that three individuals were assigned to my office. Robert B. (Stretch) Flanagan of the headquarters security office was experienced in providing necessary security arrangements and had learned to assist with public affairs activities.

The others were Roscoe Monroe, an African American school teacher who had worked for NASA's Space mobile program, and Joe Kidwell, a retired park police officer; both were of great help in our staffing needs.

Monroe and Kidwell eventually departed, and Flanagan and I would plan and staff most of the Apollo astronaut appearances between 1969 and 1975. In fact, Flanagan, who had piloted a B-25 as a U.S. Marine in the Pacific during World War II, was selected as part of the security/ public affairs staffs that accompanied both the Apollo 11 and 12 crews during their world tours.

He was also a scratch golfer, who played many rounds with several of the astronauts. Flanagan, who had acquired and preferred the name

Stretch, stood six feet four and had one peculiar life-long habit — he had grown up on a Texas ranch and refused to eat anything that flew or swam, including chicken and fish, which were often served at many functions we were staffing.

He would often snack on bread with a glass of wine (mentioning the Last Supper) rather than eat a first course serving of shrimp cocktail while waiting for the main course, which he hoped would be beef, or better yet, steak. He always requested that the steak be well done, and several times it arrived too rare and sent back to the kitchen with instructions to the chef to burn it if necessary.

We enjoyed a unique working relationship until his retirement in 1979.

In dealing with the Nixon Transition Team and working out participation for the astronauts, I learned that I would be attending the Presidential Gala at the DC Armory the evening of January 19, as the escort for the Borman's and Lovell's. Mrs. Marianetti (Peg) was invited to join me, and we scrambled to find her an appropriate evening gown. Since I never owned a tuxedo, I rented one for the occasion.

On arrival, we learned that our party would be seated with Mrs. Mamie Eisenhower and her family. It was a memorable event, with many stars performing including Singer Connie Francis, who had campaigned for Nixon and was remembered for her "Nixon is the One" TV commercial. Mrs. Eisenhower was a very gracious hostess.

On Inauguration Day, I escorted the astronauts and their wives to reserved seats at the U.S. Capitol for the swearing in of President Nixon. Following lunch and the Presidential motorcade down Pennsylvania Avenue, the astronauts and wives were seated with the President and Mrs. Nixon and family members in a specially-built Presidential Box, where they reviewed passing floats and bands. There was a big cheer as the float carrying the Apollo 7 command module and a lunar module exhibit, followed by an open car with Schirra, Eisele and Cunningham saluting as they went by.

Shortly after the Inaugural, President Nixon announced that Colonel Borman with his wife Susan and sons Frederick and Edwin would begin an eighteen-day goodwill trip on behalf of the President to England, France, Belgium, Netherlands, West Germany, Italy, Spain and Portugal.

The State Department was hopeful that all three astronauts could travel, but Lovell and Anders had already been assigned by NASA as backup members for the Apollo 11 mission scheduled to be launched in July, and would begin training soon for that mission.

Borman developed a close relationship with Nixon and key White House staffers, and upon completion of his goodwill trip, became responsible for keeping the White House informed of NASA activities before the historic Apollo 11 launch.

He later retired from the Air Force and NASA to take an administrative position with Eastern Airlines, and Anders was later appointed by Vice President Spiro Agnew as the executive secretary of the Space Council in Washington. Lovell fulfilled his role as a backup crewmember for Apollo 11, and then was named Commander of Apollo 13.

Funkhouser was selected as the NASA representative for the Borman trip. Working with the White House, State Department and the U.S. Information Agency (USIA), he was the primary escort for the astronaut party and responsible for gifts and presentations. Special Air Missions at Andrews assigned a special VC-135 aircraft and crew for the trip.

He would be missed until late February, but would figure prominently in our planning for known and unexpected events in 1969. Our work was cut out for us with the next three launches two months apart.

Plans were underway for Apollo 9, the mission originally scheduled ahead of Apollo 8, but was delayed because of problems in the development of the lunar module. It was scheduled for late February, but weather and technical problems delayed liftoff until March 3, with two veteran Gemini astronauts, Commander Jim McDivitt, command module pilot Dave Scott and rookie lunar module pilot Rusty Schweickart.

It was the first time two vehicles designed to fly and land on the Moon were successfully tested in Earth orbit and was the final step clearing the way for the next two flights with the possibility of the lunar landing, hopefully later in the year.

I always felt that the accomplishments of that flight tend to be overlooked because it was not a lunar landing mission. But without its success, the eventual landings would have been delayed and might have jeopardized President Kennedy's "Before the End of the Decade" goal. The mission lasted a little more than ten days, and McDivitt announced his retirement after the mission. Scott was later named the commander of Apollo 15, and Schweickart never flew again and eventually left the astronaut office.

Apollo 10 was a mere two months away in May with the first lunar landing attempt (Apollo 11) in July. We were faced with many problems with such a short time span between the launches. Long range planning was involved with allocation of available resources at Headquarters and the Kennedy Space Center.

Chapter Six
PRELUDE TO LUNAR LANDING

A pollo 10 will be remembered as the full dress rehearsal for Apollo 11. Tom Stafford was commander and was joined by lunar module pilot Gene Cernan and command module pilot John Young. All three had flown during Gemini, and Young will be remembered for surprising Commander Gus Grissom during the first Gemini mission, when he displayed a corn beef sandwich he had smuggled aboard. Apollo 10 also featured the crew's first use of a color television camera, which transmitted live coverage back to Earth.

Young remained in the command/service module (CSM), while Stafford and Cernan transferred to the Lunar module capsule and piloted the craft to within ten miles of the lunar surface before jettisoning the decent stage and returning in the ascent capsule and hooking up with Young in the CSM for their return to Earth. The mission lasted a little over eight days with a successful landing in the Pacific Ocean on May 26.

Everything was now in place for Apollo 11 in less than two months. The Apollo 10 crew had accomplished everything the lunar landing would require, except for the landing.

The National Academy of Television Arts and Sciences recognized the crew's use of a color TV camera during the mission and extended an invitation for the astronauts to appear at the Emmy Awards in New York and receive special Emmy's at the televised awards show on Sunday evening, June 8. An invitation was also accepted for the crew to appear that morning on the CBS Face the Nation Show.

The NASA 2 Gulfstream, based at Houston, flew the astronauts and their wives to LaGuardia on June 7. Stafford introduced me to his wife Faye, John and Barbara Young, and Gene and Barbara Cernan. We then drove in two limousines provided by the Academy to the Americana Hotel in downtown New York.

The limos would be available for us the entire weekend. We talked about a free Saturday night and Scheer, with many contacts in the entertainment world, was able to obtain complimentary tickets for the astronauts and their wives to attend a very popular Broadway show, "Promises, Promises", a Neil Simon musical/comedy starring Jerry Orbach and based on the movie, "The Apartment."

Our drive was long and slow, primarily because the Belmont Stakes, the third horserace in the Triple Crown, had been run earlier and the lobby of the hotel was packed as we waited to check in.

While waiting with our bags, Barbara Cernan pointed to a very familiar face who was noticeably irritated. It was baseball great Joe DiMaggio, who was soon joined by hotel officials and a man I would later come to know under the most unusual circumstances. It seems that the hotel had misplaced DiMaggio's reservation. Our check in went smoothly and we were escorted to our rooms.

We agreed to meet in the lobby at 7:00 that evening and leave in the limos for the short drive to the Schubert Theater and "Promises, Promises." There were only five of us, since Young and his wife had decided to skip the play and remain at the Americana.

During intermission, Cernan called me aside and suggested that I place a call to Toots Shor, who operated one of the most popular night clubs in New York, and tell him that the Apollo 10 astronauts were in town and would like to stop by for a drink.

I found the number and placed the call, which was answered by the maître d'. In just moments he was back on the line saying Toots was delighted to hear we were in town and by all means to come by.

We arrived and were greeted by none other than (you guessed it) the same man involved with Joe DiMaggio at the Americana earlier. He introduced himself as Bill Mark, a well known New York photographer, who led our group to a private booth where Toots was hosting Earl Wilson, a famous New York columnist and writer Bob Considine, co-author of the book "30 Seconds over Tokyo." He was in the process of finishing a book about Toots.

After the welcome and introductions, the astronauts and their wives slid into the booth and the group spent the rest of the evening enjoying the fine hospitality. They were soon the subject of many autograph requests once it was known that two of the three astronauts who just weeks earlier had flown to within miles of the lunar surface were there.

With the astronauts in good hands, Mark quickly introduced me to his wife Eleanor, who was seated at a nearby table, and explained the circumstances we witnessed earlier that day at the Americana. Mark was DiMaggio's personal New York representative and was called by the "Yankee Clipper" to straighten out a problem with his room reservation.

The chance meeting with Bill Mark developed into a personal/professional relationship that continued until his death in 1995. He became a strong supporter of the space program and assisted NASA's photographer Bill Taub on the many future astronaut trips to New York and Washington.

The following morning we were chauffeured to the CBS studios on West 57 Street, where the astronauts were interviewed on "Face the Nation." We returned to the Americana and were then driven to the Emmy Awards show. The crew was introduced, and each accepted an Emmy statute while receiving a standing ovation.

With the success of Apollo 10, the stage was now set for the first lunar landing attempt. The Apollo 11 crew had been selected earlier and was in training. Neil Armstrong would command the mission, with Buzz Aldrin as the lunar module pilot. But debate and rumors circulated within NASA on whether Armstrong or Aldrin would be the first to step on the lunar surface. Mike Collins was ineligible as the command module pilot.

It seemed at first it would be Aldrin, who openly campaigned for the honor, but about three months before the scheduled Apollo 11 liftoff it was announced that it would be Armstrong. NASA's explanation was that Armstrong, as the commander, would have a clear path to exit the LM and it made more sense for him to exit first as the commander and senior member of the crew.

Another argument that NASA refuted was that the first man on the Moon should be a civilian. Aldrin was U.S. Air Force Colonel while Armstrong, a civilian, had served during the Korean War as a U.S. Navy Lieutenant pilot (junior grade). It was thought within NASA management that Neil's ego made him better equipped and that he also outranked Aldrin by a year in seniority.

Chapter Seven

MAJOR PLANNING AND THE BIG LAUNCH

F ollowing the New York trip, I returned to Washington and resumed working with St. Clair to complete arrangements for the Apollo 11 launch six weeks away on July 16. Scheer and St. Clair determined that I should make plans to leave for Florida in late June.

For me it was a work assignment, but we could also make it a family vacation and the chance for all of us to see history in the making. Peg, sons Randy, Mickey and daughters Jamie and Kelly, born on election night in 1968, would accompany me. The plan was for them to enjoy the beach while I worked. We left by car on June 28 following the boy's little league game, and drove to Florence, South Carolina, where we spent our first night.

I had acquired a Ford Torino earlier that year and our boys and daughter Jamie shared the backseat, arguing who would have the window seats, while Peg rode with me up front. Kelly had her own car seat, which was straddled between us with her own steering wheel. We recall the experience and realize it could never happen again because of the many car safety improvements, including being strapped in a car seat.

Large blocks of rooms in Cocoa Beach, Orlando, Melbourne, and as far at Daytona Beach, had been reserved for guests at their own expense. I was fortunate to have a room at the Beach Motel, right on the Atlantic Ocean. It came equipped with a kitchenette and a bunk bed and served our needs well during the three weeks we were there. With my government per Diem, our out of pocket costs were minimal, and the family was able to enjoy the beach and getting to know the families of other NASA workers there for the launch.

We had determined early in our planning that the Cocoa Beach Guest Center would be inadequate to handle the anticipated thousands of guests for the first lunar landing launch, so satellite guest centers would be opened in nearby Titusville, Cocoa, Melbourne and Orlando and Daytona Beach.

I had the primary responsibility for the day-to-day operation of the Cocoa Beach Guest Center, and coordination between the satellite centers. St. Clair was working with the U.S. Secret Service, Kennedy Space Center personnel and the White House in arranging for former President Lyndon B. Johnson and his family to observe the launch as guests of President Nixon. Funkhouser was coordinating the NASA Administrator's schedule, which included arranging for several charter aircraft to fly Washington dignitaries to the launch.

Special guest viewing sites were erected, complete with portable toilets, bleachers and a sound system with launch commentary from the launch center adjacent to the huge Vehicle Assembly Building. Jack King, the KSC public information officer stationed in Launch Control, provided the launch countdown commentary.

As the launch day approached, the central Florida area was inundated with thousands of people. Most had arrived without invitations, but were content to find and stake out viewing locations on the beaches or along the roads leading to Cape Kennedy.

All the municipal jurisdictions within Brevard County, especially Cape Canaveral, Cocoa, Cocoa Beach and Titusville, worked closely with NASA to provide necessary resources (portable toilets, drinking water and first aid facilities in parking lots and roadways. Local radio stations agreed to broadcast the launch countdown, which enabled thousands to see the liftoff and listen on their car radios to countdown commentary.

Those who were able to obtain special guest invitations were bused from the many guest centers to viewing sites three and a half miles from Launch Pad 39-A, while other NASA guests and the general public obtained car and bus passes, which enabled them to drive on to the NASA Causeway and view the launch from about seven miles away. While not as close to the actual liftoff, the Causeway provided a much better view of the Saturn V as it roared to life and began staging down range.

I had left our motel room very early that morning for the short drive to our guest center in the Cape Royal Building on North Atlantic Avenue in Cocoa Beach. Guests were already arriving and began boarding charter buses for the estimated one to two hour drive to the special guest viewing site.

Meanwhile, three charter and four NASA Gulfstream aircraft departed Washington, Houston and Huntsville early that morning and were met by buses and escorts and driven across the NASA Causeway (which separates NASA and the Air Force Station at Cape Canaveral) to the special guest viewing sites.

Aboard the charter aircraft from Washington were sixty-nine ambassadors, Supreme Court justices, Cabinet members and other Washington dignitaries. The President had invited every member of Congress and the fifty state governors, nineteen of whom were there. *Life Magazine* had flown in the presidents of the fifty largest U.S. companies, and a French charter landed in nearby Melbourne, carrying U.S. Ambassador to France Sergeant Shriver and eighty high ranking European industrialists.

Also in attendance were the mayors of forty U.S. cities and many celebrities including Johnny Carson and Jack Benny. Although invited, Senator Ted Kennedy and other members of the Kennedy family did not attend and missed the opportunity to witness the fulfillment of President Kennedy's 1961 challenge "to land a man on the Moon and return him safely to Earth."

President Nixon was at the Cape the night before the launch where he had dinner with the three astronauts in the Crew Quarters before flying back to Washington immediately afterwards. Vice President Agnew arrived about 10 o'clock that night, stayed at a private residence overnight, and was flown by helicopter to the special guest viewing site the following morning where he was seated next to former President and Lady Bird Johnson, who were personal guests of President Nixon.

The launch countdown was proceeding normally on an unusually hot and humid morning, and they and the many thousands there rose to their feet as the Saturn V engines ignited and roared to life as Jack King, the NASA PAO commentator in Launch Control, delivered his now famous, "3, 2, 1, we have a liftoff, 32 minutes past the hour" at 9:32 a.m., as the 363 foot rocket with 7.5 million pounds of thrust, gently lifted off the launch pad and the three astronauts were on their way to a place in history.

After being sent toward the Moon by the Saturn V's upper stage, the astronauts separated the spacecraft from it and traveled for three days until they entered lunar orbit. Armstrong and Aldrin then moved into the lunar module (LM) and landed in the Sea of Tranquility with about 25 seconds of fuel remaining at 4:17 p.m. Eastern Time on July 20, 1969, five months ahead of President Kennedy's deadline.

It seemed an eternity until Armstrong's confirmation to Mission Control, "Tranquility Base Here, the *Eagle* has landed."

Of course, millions watched on live TV as Armstrong took the first step from the LM *Eagle* at 10:56 p.m. Eastern Time with the famous, "That's one small step for a man, one giant leap for mankind". A stainless steel plaque attached to a leg on *Eagle* read, "Here men from the planet Earth first set foot upon the Moon, July 1969 A.D. We came in peace for all mankind."

Aldrin followed Armstrong down the ladder about nineteen minutes later. Millions watched from a small black and white camera as the two planted an American flag in the lunar soil, collected rocks and samples, deployed a scientific package, and received a congratulatory call from President Nixon from the White House. Viewers were able to watch and listen on a split TV screen.

The TV camera continued to capture the historic moments and televise live pictures around the world. Surprisingly, Armstrong carried the lone Hasselblad 500 EL and snapped all the lunar surface shots. The Hasselblad cameras aboard were medium formatted, using 70 mm film loaded in magazines.

After about 21 hours on the lunar surface, the crew lifted off in *Eagle*'s upper stage and rejoined command module pilot Michael Collins in the orbiting *Columbia* CSM and the return to Earth, splashing down about 900 miles southwest of Hawaii in the North Pacific Ocean on July 24, where they were recovered and transferred to the Mobile Quarantine Facility (MQF).

President Nixon and Acting NASA Administrator Thomas Paine were aboard the recovery ship USS *Hornet* to welcome the crew back to Earth. Nixon spoke briefly before the *Hornet* sailed to Pearl Harbor, where the crew inside the MQF was loaded aboard a C-141 aircraft and flown to Houston where they would remain in quarantine.

As I write this less than a year before the 50th anniversary, the movie "First Man" based on the life of Armstrong and from the book of the same name by Professor James R. Hansen, has received wide acclaim at showings at the Venice and Toronto film festivals. It opened at U.S. theaters on October 12 to mixed reviews. However, Canadian actor Ryan Gosling, who plays the role of Armstrong in the movie, has defended the decision to delete the planting of the American Flag by Armstrong and Aldrin in the film saying the landing was not just an American victory but transcended countries and borders, although the flag is seen throughout the movie. Neil's sons Rick and Mark have defended the move, while Aldrin has slammed the decision and quoted as saying he was proud to be an American. U.S. Senator Marco Rubio of Florida, called the decision "total lunacy" and a disservice at a time when people need reminders of what we can achieve when we work together, saying American people paid for that mission, on rockets built by Americans, with American technology and carrying American Astronauts. It wasn't a UN mission.

I saw the movie and while I attempted to keep an open mind, I personally felt the filmmakers could have avoided controversy by showing a brief segment of the actual planting during the more than two-hour plus movie. I will say that I think we more than recognized Apollo 11 as a human achievement with the words on the plaque left by the astronauts: "Here Men from the Planet Earth First Set Foot Upon the Moon July 1969 AD. We Came in Peace for all Mankind. Even Neil's famous words, "That's One Small Step for a Man, One Giant Leap for Mankind" was his way of confirming the event as a human achievement."

I believe most Americans view the scene much the same way they take pride in Americans planting the Stars and Stripes on Iwo Jima. Both were proud moments in the history of our country!

Chapter Eight

SETTING RECORDS WITH THE
SATURN MOON LAUNCHES

I had extended a launch invitation to Ray Fenton, an old Montana friend who was the publisher of the *Montana Rural Electric News Magazine.* Knowing the many NASA contributions to agriculture, Fenton felt it important to attend the launch and learn more about the space agency.

Following the launch, Ray flew to Washington and was at our home in Alexandria, Virginia, the afternoon of July 20, where we sat glued to the TV and held our collective breath as Neil Armstrong and Buzz Aldrin piloted the LM *Eagle* to a landing on the Sea of Tranquility.

Ray was able to photograph the entire sequences with his camera from our living room and his firsthand account, complete with photos, was the centerpiece story in the September 1969 issue of the *Montana Rural Electric News.*

Worldwide interest in the history-making event resulted in a record number of 3,000 media representatives from fifty-six foreign countries and all the major U.S. TV networks and newspapers. It's estimated that the Apollo 11 launch attracted an estimated 750,000 people, while some 530 million watched around the world on TV.

By the time the program ended in 1972 with the nighttime liftoff of Apollo 17, an estimated six million had witnessed the nine Saturn V Moon launches in person, and that didn't include the untold thousands who lined the roads leading to the space center.

Never in U.S. history had a U.S. Government agency devoted so much time and energy to ensure that the public would have reasonable access to a national program they were paying and supporting with tax dollars.

For NASA, the guest invitation program was the fulfillment of a requirement created by The Space Act of 1958, which mandated the agency provide "the widest practicable and appropriate dissemination of information concerning its activities."

Back in Washington, we were already at work mapping out a post-flight appearance schedule. We began to review and evaluate the hundreds of requests from around the country and the world. The top priority originated with the President.

We soon learned that he would honor the astronauts at a state dinner, the first ever held outside the White House, at the Century Plaza Hotel in Los Angeles on August 13, just three days after their release from quarantine. The White House emphasized that nothing was to interfere with the President's dinner, and they should arrive in Los Angeles no later than 5:30pm PDT.

Scheer began coordinating with the White House, and was finally able to get approval for the astronauts to participate in ticker tape parades and honor award ceremonies in New York City and Chicago on August 13, but only with the assurance that they would be in Los Angeles by 5:30. The President made available his Air Force One for the trip.

Even with the use of Air Force One and Time Zone changes, it would be difficult but could be accomplished. We immediately assembled a staffing plan for all three events. St. Clair and I departed for Houston with responsibility for overall coordination of the New York, Chicago and State Dinner events. Scheer would be the senior NASA official aboard the aircraft, but his primary focus was to conduct the crew's first meeting with the media in Houston.

Bill Lloyd, the NASA veteran of previous astronaut visits to New York, was dispatched there to coordinate the details with the staffs of Governor Rockefeller, Mayor John Lindsay and the United Nations. Ed Pierce, as he had done with Apollo 8, left for Chicago, and Jim Funkhouser would be the senior NASA representative at the Century Plaza.

His was probably the most difficult assignment, dealing with the White House, secret service, members of Congress, the diplomatic corps, the hotel management and staff and the family and friends of the astronauts and having to resolve some impossible requests.

St. Clair and I arrived in Houston on August 5, set up a command post at the Manned Spacecraft Center, and were in constant phone conversations with Lloyd, Pierce and Funkhouser in developing an overall minute by minute schedule beginning with the takeoff in Houston, and ending with landing in Los Angeles on August 13.

We did have one opportunity to brief the crew during the quarantine for the events on August 13. A day following their release, we met for a more detailed briefing for the three astronauts and their families at Neil and Janet Armstrong's home in Houston.

We also informed them that they would be making a world tour on behalf of the President, but that dates and locations were in talking stages and that they would be kept informed as details became available. President Nixon would make the official announcement at the State Dinner.

It was August 12 before details had been finalized, and we were ready for what we knew would be a hectic, but historic, day. Air Force One, the President's 707, landed at Ellington Air Force Base near the NASA Manned Spacecraft Center on August 12.

Chapter Nine

HONORING THE FIRST MOONWALKERS

T he astronaut party was welcomed aboard the aircraft, and it was wheels up about 5:00 a.m. the following morning. The plane's commander, Lt. Colonel Peden, had calculated an on-time arrival in New York and we touched down at John F. Kennedy International Airport, where they were welcomed by Mayor John Lindsay and his wife, Mary.

The landing party then boarded helicopters for the short flight to a pier near Wall Street, where the astronauts boarded the first in a line of open convertibles with their families and support staff following.

Ticker tape parades were nothing new for New York City, and more than 205 honoring individuals had been held dating back to 1886. Aviators Charles Lindbergh and Amelia Earhart were honored after their record-breaking achievements, as well as General Douglas MacArthur in 1951.

John Glenn and Gordon Cooper were the first astronauts to be so honored and were followed by the Apollo 8 crew in 1969. But this one honoring the first Moon-landing crew is believed to be the largest ever as millions lined Broadway and the route to City Hall.

Mayor Lindsay, as he had done a few months earlier for the Apollo 8 astronauts, presented each with City of New York Medals, followed by brief remarks from the three astronauts including presentation of a framed plaque with a flown U.S. flag and Apollo patch.

The astronaut party was soon back in convertibles for the drive to the United Nations, where they were welcomed by Secretary General U Thant, who presented the astronauts with books of commemorative stamps representing the countries of all UN members. Neil spoke on behalf of the crew and presented the Secretary-General with an Apollo 11 gift.

Our departure from JFK International was slightly behind schedule, but with a one-hour time change in our favor, Colonel Peden

James Webb, NASA's second administrator. President Kennedy, with the assistance of Vice-President Johnson, had to convince Webb that he was the right man for NASA. He served as Administrator from 1961-68 and is credited as the man most responsible for achieving the first lunar landing.

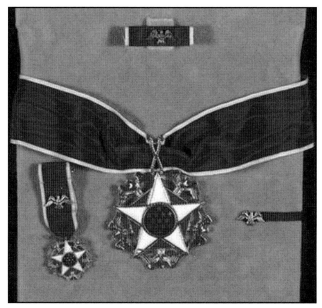

James Webb received many awards and accolades for his service with NASA, including the Presidential Medal of Freedom in 1969, the nation's highest civilian honor.

Bill Taub, who produced thousands of photographs during his career with NASA.

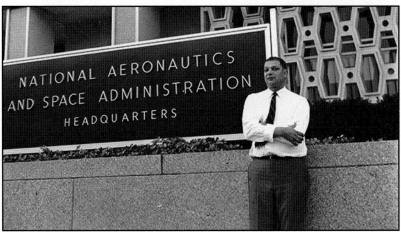

Julian Scheer, photographed in front of NASA Headquarters in Washington, D.C., shortly after he was appointed by NASA Administrator James Webb to be Assistant Administrator for Public Affairs.

The crew of Apollo 1, Gus Grissom, Ed White, and Roger Chaffee.

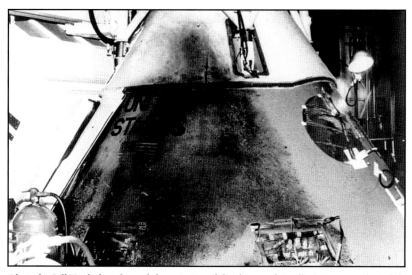

Photo by Bill Taub that showed the exterior of the damaged Apollo 1 Command Module following the devastating fire of January 27, 1967.

A NASA Space Mobile, one of many mobile units equipped with models and space-related exhibits manned by teachers who traveled and conducted workshops at selected schools.

The Original 7 Mercury Astronauts pose for photographer Bill Taub in front of a jet at Patrick Air Force Base, January 20, 1961. Pictured l-r: Scott Carpenter, Gordon Cooper, John Glenn, Gus Grissom, Wally Schirra, Alan Shepard, and Deke Slayton.

President John F. Kennedy gives his famous speech to members of the U.S. Congress in 1961, during which he issued his challenge to land a man on the Moon and return him safely to Earth within a decade.

John Glenn boards the Friendship 7 *spacecraft in 1962.*

A T-38 supersonic jet trainer flown by the astronauts for years to maintain flight efficiency, but also to travel to and from public appearances when available.

The success of the first unmanned Saturn V launch (Apollo 4) paved the way for its use on every lunar launch that followed.

Official Apollo 7 patch.

Veteran Mercury and Gemini astronaut Wally Schirra, flanked by rookies Donn Eisele on his right and Walt Cunningham on the left, commanded the first manned Apollo 7 mission in 1968.

Official Apollo 8 patch.

The Apollo 8 crew (l-r): Commander Frank Borman, William Anders, and James Lovell, first men to break the bonds of Earth, fly to and orbit the Moon, Christmas 1968.

The launch of Apollo 8 on December 21, 1968.

Famous picture of the Earth rising as the crew of Apollo 8 circle the Moon, December 1968. Photo taken by Astronaut Bill Anders

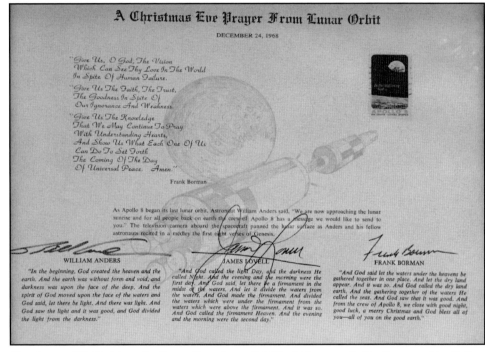

Signed copy of "A Christmas Eve Prayer From Lunar Orbit", which was recited by the crew of Apollo 8 on December 24, 1968.

James E. Webb and President John F. Kennedy.

The NASA management team responsible for working with Congress to obtain the necessary funds to support the Apollo program. Pictured l-r: Dr. Robert Seamans, Webb, George Mueller, Manned Space Flight Administrator and Apollo Program Director General Samuel Phillips.

Astronaut Frank Borman speaks before a joint meeting of Congress to describe his experiences aboard Apollo 8 and one of the first three men to orbit the Moon.

Governor Nelson Rockefeller of New York presents the members of Apollo 8 with Gold Medals.

Apollo 8 motorcade in New York City, NY.

Apollo 8 astronauts and their wives visit the United Nations during their public relations trip to New York City.

The author (standing to the right of Jim Lovell) rides along with the crew of Apollo 8 - Lovell, Borman and Anders - during a parade in Chicago, Illinois, June 15, 1969. The photograph is autographed by Lovell.

Nixon Inaugural Parade

New York tickertape parade for the crew of Apollo 11, August 13, 1969.

Robert B. (Stretch) Flanagan of the NASA security office with Gene prior to an astronaut appearnce in New York City.

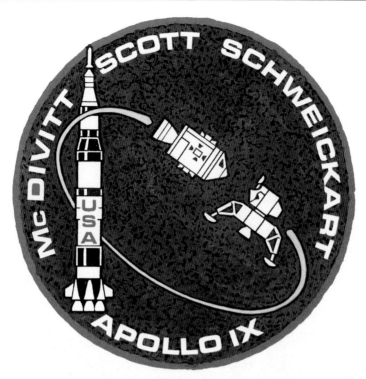

Apollo 9 Patch

Crew of Apollo 9. Pictured l-r: James A. McDivitt, David R. Scott, and Russell L. Sch-weickart.

Apollo 10 Patch

Crew of Apollo 10. Pictured l-r: Eugene A. Cernan, Thomas P. Stafford, and John W. Young.

Members of Apollo 10 pose with their Emmy awards.

New York photographer Bill Mark snapped this photo of (l-r) Earl Wilson, Barbara Cernan, Tom Stafford, (wife Faye being kissed by Toots Shor), Gene Cernan and Bob Considine, June 1969.

Apollo 11 Patch

Crew of Apollo 11. Pictured l-r: Neil Armstrong, Michael Collins, and Buzz Aldrin.

Apollo 11 lifts off at Cape Canaveral, Florida, July 16, 1969.

Photo of Buzz Aldrin on the Moon. Neil Armstrong took this photograph and his image and the Eagle LM *is reflected in Aldrin's helmet visor.*

President Richard Nixon welcomes the Apollo 11 astronauts while they recover in the Mobile Quarantine Facility aboard the USS Hornet, July 24, 1969.

Houston honored the three astronauts who rode in open convertibles on August 16, 1969 as part of the Houston hometown welcome. The three rode together in a single car in both New York and Chicago.

73

Houston honored the three astronauts who rode in open convertibles on August 16, 1969 as part of the Houston hometown welcome. The three rode together in a single car in both New York and Chicago. Pictured here are Buzz Aldrin and his wife, Joan.

Neil, with sons Mark and Rick, receive warm welcome in Wapakoneta motorcade during hometown welcome on September 6, 1969.

Neil, wife Janet and sons Mark and Rick, acknowledge welcome during Houston hometown motorcade, August 16, 1969.

Mike Collins during a New Orleans welcome.

The Apollo 11 motorcade in New York.

The intersection of Michigan and Chicago during the Chicago ticker tape celebration for Apollo 11.

Neil Armstrong prepares to pilot a helicopter during a tour of German aircraft facilities.

Wives of the Apollo 11 astronauts happily take a break from the madness during the Apollo 11 tour.

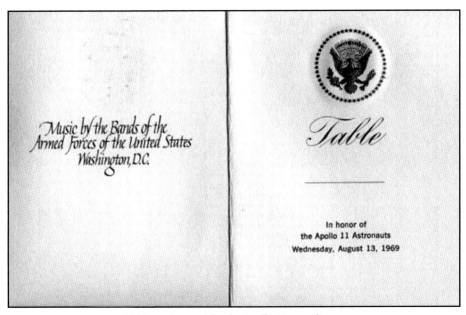

Music by the Bands of the Armed Forces of the United States Washington, D.C.

Table

In honor of
the Apollo 11 Astronauts
Wednesday, August 13, 1969

Table seating card for the Apollo 11 state dinner.

DINNER
In honor of the
Apollo 11 Astronauts

Wente Brothers
Pinot Chardonnay

Supreme of Salmon Commodore

Filet of Beef Perigourdine

Inglenook)
Cabernet Sauvignon
Cask,

Artichauds Columbia

Carottes Des Indes

Limestone Lettuce

Fromages de Brie, Bel Paese,

Korbel
Natural

Roquefort

Clair de Lune

CENTURY PLAZA
Los Angeles, California
Wednesday, August 13, 1969

Menu for the Presidential state dinner in honor of the Apollo 11 astronauts.

was confident he would have us in Chicago on time. His calculations were right on target and he covered the 675 air miles in an hour and 35 minutes.

Air Force One, with that beautiful color scheme emblazoned with "United States of America," touched down at O'Hare International Airport and taxied to a designated area, where the astronauts were welcomed by Mayor Richard Daley. The motorcade then departed for downtown Chicago, where an estimated 2 million people jammed the parade route.

The *Chicago Tribune* reported:" It was more than a parade, it was glory. The brilliant blue sky was filled with ticker tape that seemed without source, streets and avenues were no longer thoroughfares but masses of humanity, and the cheers, the sirens, the ringing bells created so great a din that no other sound could be heard."

The packed seven-mile motorcade along State Street and Michigan Avenue ended with a ceremony at City Hall, where Daley made welcoming remarks and presented the astronauts with keys to the city and large engraved sterling silver punch bowls followed by remarks by the astronauts.

The plan called for the motorcade to return to O'Hare, but Daley had arranged for thousands of school children to gather in Lincoln Park, where the motorcade stopped and the astronauts delivered brief remarks.

The clock was running, and while the astronauts were basking in the warm welcome, it became necessary to move things along and get back on schedule. The drive back was slower than usual because of the thousands who continued to pack the parade route, and we were running late.

Our plane was waiting, and we were soon airborne for the final leg of the flight on this whirlwind day. Lt. Colonel Peden and his crew were working frantically to make up the lost time and informed us that it would take an estimated 3 hours and 35 minutes to reach Los Angeles and would be close to arriving on time.

The astronauts and their families, along with the NASA support staff, were finally able to relax and enjoy a specially prepared lunch. The flight time provided Scheer and St. Clair an opportunity to discuss with the astronauts some of the details about the President's planed world tour that would be announced at the State Dinner that night.

At the same time I was able to meet with the three wives to discuss the roles they were expected to play in the days and months ahead.

Since all three of their husbands had flown on Gemini missions, the wives were familiar with media and public interest, but realized they would be experiencing much more exposure from an admiring public and expressed concern about the media demands at each stop on the road.

Apollo 8 Commander Frank Borman, who had been serving as NASA's liaison with the White House on matters related to Apollo 11, was at the Century Plaza and called Scheer at least twice to check on our flight status and to emphasize the importance of an on time arrival.

Helicopters were standing by at Los Angeles International Airport upon our arrival to transport the astronaut party to the parking lot of the Century Plaza Hotel in Beverly Hills. Los Angeles Mayor Sam Yorty was there for an official welcome, and presented the astronauts with keys to the city and flowers to the wives.

Funkhouser, along with Stretch Flanagan and Joe Kidwell from my office, were at the hotel along with a security detail to escort the party to their rooms and to prepare for the dinner.

The *Los Angeles Times* had billed the State Dinner, the first ever held outside the White House, as "one of the largest, most prestigious and most publicized state dinners in history."

More than 1,400 people attended and included future President and current California Governor Ronald Reagan and wife Nancy; all but six of the other state governors, fifty members of Congress, fourteen Cabinet members, Chief Supreme Court Justice and Mrs. Warren Burger, Mamie Eisenhower, former Vice President and Mrs. Hubert Humphrey, Barry Goldwater, Wernher von Braun, Billy Graham, and diplomats from eighty-three nations. Celebrities included Bob Hope, Jimmy Stewart, Red Skelton, Buddy Rodgers and Gene Autry. Other guests included astronaut family members and their guests, Jimmy Doolittle and other space and aviation pioneers.

The program included remarks from the President and Vice President and responses from the astronauts before they were presented with Presidential Medals of Freedom. The President also used the occasion to announce that the astronauts would be making an around the world tour named "Giantstep" on his behalf.

As a memento of the historic event, each guest received a commemorative plaque matching the one left on the lunar surface by Armstrong and Aldrin. It says, "Here men from the planet Earth first set foot upon the Moon July 1969, A.D. We came in peace for all mankind."

I said at the outset that Funkhouser had the most difficult assignment of all the public affairs personnel. He was the senior NASA representative at the Century Plaza for over a week and the recipient of requests and impossible demands of hotel personnel, the White House, and staffers from members of Congress, and the diplomatic corps.

He had to also contend with hundreds of anti-war demonstrators outside the hotel and the highly publicized Charles Manson murders, which were occurring prior to our arrival. He had received numerous anonymous calls threatening the lives of the astronauts. Of course, each call had to be taken seriously and investigated by the Secret Service.

In the weeks following the dinner, NASA began receiving requests from the Century Plaza to take care of many unpaid bills that invited dinner guests had assumed would be paid for by NASA. While many were eventually settled, I understand that the NASA Administrator's Fund took care of the rest.

The next morning we boarded our plane for the return flight to Ellington Air Force Base, where NASA staff cars were waiting to drive the astronauts to their homes. Next on the schedule was the city of Houston's welcome two days later on Saturday, August 16.

Crowds estimated at more than 300,000 lined the Houston parade route, as each of the three astronauts rode in open convertibles to a luncheon at the Rice Hotel. The celebration concluded that evening with a grand performance for some 45,000 packed in the Houston Astrodome. Frank Sinatra was the master of ceremonies and of course sang "Fly Me to the Moon." Also there were comedians Flip Wilson and Bill Dana, along with singers Dionne Warwick and Nancy Ames.

Back in Washington, we continued working on the many Apollo 11 events remaining before the start of the "Giantstep," tour, September 29 through November 5. The Vice President's Boeing 707 aircraft was made available for the trip. The astronauts would visit twenty-two countries in thirty-eight days. Scheer and St. Clair's first priority was to select a support staff that would be part of the traveling party.

The overall mission director for the tour would be Nick Ruwe, the deputy chief of protocol for the State Department, with Scheer as deputy mission director and St. Clair the responsibility of assisting and supervising staffers from NASA, State Department, U.S. Information

Agency and communicating with advance teams who were leap-fogging the tour city-by-city. Their advance work was critical in the success of each stop because of arrival arrangements, security and motorcade assignments.

Geneva Barnes, who began her NASA career in 1962 and was associated with agency special events and ceremonies, was selected as a member of the support staff making the trip. Stretch Flanagan, Joe Kidwell from my office, and NASA photographer Bill Taub were the others.

Scheer and St. Clair were aware that "Giantstep" would effectively remove them from the day-to-day public affairs activities back home, and it was determined that Funkhouser would assume St. Clair's role with assistance from me. I of course would be without Flanagan and Kidwell, but my other staff members, including Roscoe Monroe, Gloria Todd and Tawana Clary, would fill in admirably, and they did.

Chapter Ten

MORE COMMITMENTS FROM THE CREW OF APOLLO 11

B ut before the start of "Giantstep", there remained other Apollo 11 crew commitments. The Apollo 12 launch was still about three months away, but we had already started preliminary planning and it was rumored that President Nixon would be attending.

At hand immediately were requests from Wapakoneta, Ohio, Neil's home town and Montclair, New Jersey for Buzz. Mike, who was born in Rome, joked that he would be delighted to celebrate a return and he soon learned that New Orleans wanted to honor him, but he graciously declined saying he was not a native son.

However, he was reminded that he owed powerful Louisiana Congressman Eddy Hebert for his appointment to West Point years earlier and it was payback time. Mike finally agreed and received a traditional "Welcome Home" reception. We were able to confirm all three hometown visits for Saturday, September 6, 1969.

I had been working with city and state officials for Neil's welcome home in Wapakoneta, Ohio, while other PAO representatives were handling arrangements for Buzz Aldrin in his hometown of Montclair, New Jersey, also famous for being the home of New York Yankee great Yogi Berra.

A NASA Gulfstream flew Aldrin, wife Joan and the three Aldrin children to Newark, where the welcome home activities included a stop at the YWCA building where Buzz returned a YWCA pin he had carried to the moon. There was a brief press conference in the library of Montclair State College, followed by a parade that concluded at the Montclair high school stadium.

The welcome concluded that night with a banquet in the cafeteria dining room of Montclair State College, which included the surprise presentation and retirement of Adrian's number 28 High School Football Jersey and the unveiling of a plaque at the original home of Buzz and the Aldrin family.

Funkhouser and Mack Herring, from the NASA Mississippi Test Facility, would provide staffing assistance for Collins, who rode in an open car down Canal Street and received a warm welcome from the thousands who lined the streets.

Mayor Victor Schiro hosted a luncheon, where Collins proudly claimed New Orleans as his adopted home town. That night he attended an NFL exhibition game between his hometown Houston Oilers and the host New Orleans Saints.

Our legislative affairs office was already working with Senate and House leadership on the arrangements for the three astronauts to address a joint meeting of Congress on Tuesday, September 16, and would be virtually the same as the one held for the Apollo 8 astronauts earlier that year.

Meanwhile, a committee was already planning a hometown welcome and Neil and I discussed the details by phone. We agreed on a general schedule of events that would include a motorcade and a ceremony at the fairgrounds.

By the time I arrived in Wapakoneta days before the event, Neil's brother Dean was of great help in the final planning. Cleveland native Bob Hope would be the parade marshal and serve as the MC for the main event at the fairgrounds.

The planning committee was comprised of local and state officials, and I found myself caught in the middle of a potential problem that I brought to Neil's attention. It was our understanding that the Wapakoneta celebration was to welcome and honor a native son and world hero. But some members of the planning committee representing Ohio Governor James Rhodes, wanted to use the event to raise funds for a proposed a museum as a monument to the achievements of not only Armstrong but all Ohioans, such as the Wright Brothers, John Glenn, and others who contributed to advancement of aerospace.

The state of Ohio pledged $500,000, and Rhodes challenged the local community to match dollar for dollar, the funds to build the museum in Wapakoneta. When told the plan, Neil strongly objected and wanted it understood that he had agreed to return to Wapakoneta to be honored as a native son, and would not attend unless the matter was settled.

I conveyed Neil's concerns to the Governor's representatives, making it clear he would not endorse or allow use of his name in the effort. It finally became necessary for me to call Scheer and explain the problem.

He quickly discussed the matter with NASA's general counsel who called Governor Rhodes office warning that continued use of Armstrong's name in the effort would be a violation of federal law. Neil made it clear to me that he was there to be honored by his hometown and was embarrassed that the state was attempting to use the event as a fundraiser.

Ironically, local residents eventually met the challenge and even without Neil's endorsement or support, were able to raise over half of the total cost. The museum opened on July 20, 1972, and Neil joined Patricia Nixon, representing her father, in the presentation of an Apollo 11 lunar rock for permanent display.

A NASA Gulfstream carrying Neil and Janet and the young Armstrong boys Rick and Mark touched down at the Wapakoneta airport and following brief welcoming remarks, were transported to the home of Neil's parents Stephen and Viola, with the Armstrong boys Rick and Mark and wife Janet.

The hometown welcome included a motorcade, in which Neil rode in an open car with his boys Rick and Mark and wife Janet as he waved to adoring crowds who filled the red, white and blue bunting lined streets and watched from roof tops as the caravan, led by Bob Hope, traveled the parade route to the fairgrounds where the bleachers were filled to capacity.

Hope entertained the crowd and had help from Ed McMahon and Phyllis Diller. The high school band, of which Neil had been a member, provided the entertainment and Neil's welcome home speech included, "I am proud to stand before you today and consider myself one of you."

When the official events had ended, I accompanied the Armstrong's to the home of his brother Dean, where I joined a small group for a belated birthday celebration for Neil, who had observed his 39th birthday on August 5, while he was still in quarantine. It was a relaxing way to end the day and we enjoyed drinks and finger foods.

Chapter Eleven

AROUND THE WORLD IN
THIRTY-EIGHT DAYS

W ith the hometown celebrations behind them, the astronauts flew
to Washington for two appearances on Tuesday, September 9.
The first was at the U.S. Post Office Building in Washington to unveil a
stamp commemorating the first lunar landing. Noted artist Paul Calle
had drawn a depiction of Neil stepping down onto the lunar surface,
and the caption "First Man on the Moon." Neil and Buzz had carried
a special die to the Moon that was used to make the stamp's printing
plates. The two then personally postmarked the stamp.

The three astronauts smiled along with Postmaster General Malcolm Blount as the stamp was unveiled, and their initial thoughts were
that Calle had beautifully captured the moment of Neil stepping off the
lunar ladder onto the lunar surface.

What disturbed Neil somewhat, but especially Buzz, was the caption beneath the stamp, "First Man on the Moon." In later remarks,
Neil said the lunar landing was a two-man effort and that Buzz should
be recognized for his part in the accomplishment.

It is widely felt that use of "Men" rather than "Man" would have
been more appropriate for the oversized colorful 10 Cent stamp, the
largest the U.S. had issued to that time.

One final appearance remained before the crew's joint appearance
before Congress on Tuesday, September 16, which would be followed
a week later by their historic "Giantstep" world tour. The astronauts
would be guests of honor at a NASA Splashdown Party at the Shore-
ham Hotel in Washington.

The affair filled the hotel's large ballroom with a guest list that
included top NASA officials and employees from Washington and
agency field centers, and representatives from the many contractors
who provided the launch and spacecraft hardware for the Apollo
program.

The astronauts were the last to speak after speeches by senior NASA officials Acting Administrator Dr. T.O. Paine and Lt. General Sam Phillips, the Apollo program director. Mike spoke first and was followed by Buzz and Neil, who gave the closing remarks.

Each attendee was given a commemorative dinner program containing the "We Came in Peace for All Mankind" plaque the crew left on the Moon along with a cancelled first day of issue of the lunar stamp. I was fortunate to have illustrator Paul Calle sign my copy.

Twenty-years later, his stamp designer, son Chris, produced a special first day of issue Priority Mail Moon Landing Stamp for the U.S. Postal Service to honor the historic achievement commemorating the 20th anniversary of the first lunar landing, which President George H.W. Bush and Postmaster General Anthony Frank dedicated.

The astronauts and their families were staying at the Georgetown Inn on Wisconsin Avenue, where they were comfortable with the accommodations and its location to official events. We had a good working relationship with the proprietor Collins Byrd, thanks to St. Clair.

Byrd had been more than accommodating two years earlier for astronauts and families attending funeral services at Arlington National Cemetery for Gus Grissom and Roger Chaffee.

The astronauts, and especially the wives, were anxious to return to Houston and begin preparations for the world tour. But still remaining on the schedule was the crew's appearance before a joint meeting of Congress on Tuesday, September 16.

Discussions about the scheduled "Giantstep" trip continued to dominate conversations and many of the questions and details about the trip would be answered at State Department briefing on September 10.

The astronauts and their wives were presented with briefing books, and it was there they learned that they would be visiting twenty-two countries in thirty-eight days beginning in Mexico City on September 29.

Speech writers with years of experience writing for the administrator and other officials were available to help with suggested remarks before Congress, but all three astronauts worked diligently alone preparing remarks that expressed gratitude for the opportunity of representing the people of the United States in one of mankind's greatest achievements.

Neil had been working on his speech by hand writing his thoughts on stationary, when he inquired about a typewriter and typist. I could type about 32 words a minute on an old manual typewriter and offered to type it for him. We located a typewriter, and I was able to type the speech he would deliver the next day.

I often think back of that experience and recall that I learned to type in high school because it was essential for a journalism career. Little did I realize then that I would be using my nimble fingers to type from hand written notes a speech to be delivered to Congress by the first man to step foot on the Moon.

All three astronauts delivered brief, but eloquent, remarks and Neil concluded the ceremony with two presentations, saying, "We carried on Apollo 11 two flags of this Union that had flown over the Capitol, one over the House of Representatives, one over the Senate. It is our privilege to return them now in these halls, which exemplify man's highest purpose — to serve one's fellow man.

We thank you, on behalf of all the men of Apollo, for giving us the privilege of joining you in serving — mankind." The flags were presented to the Speaker of the House and to the Vice President.

They then returned to Houston to prepare for the overseas trip that the White House billed as an opportunity for the astronauts to share their experiences with the people of world. It would be the first of several foreign trips by returning Apollo astronauts between 1969 and 1973.

The 707 aircraft was in place at Andrews Air Force Base early the morning of September 29, when Scheer, St. Clair, Stretch Flanagan, Joe Kidwell, NASA photographer Bill Taub and Geneva Barnes, who was responsible for clerical support, boarded the aircraft for the flight to Ellington Air Force Base, near Houston where the astronauts, wives and other support members would be waiting and ready to begin the world tour beginning in Mexico City.

A well documented personal diary of the entire trip was written by Ms. Barnes and published in the book "Before This Decade Is Out" and contains personal reflections of the Apollo program and is available from the U.S. Government Printing Office (NASA SP:4223 - The NASA History Series.)

We received occasional cables and phone calls from the plane reporting on the various stops, but Funkhouser and I found ourselves busy planning guest operations for the Apollo 12 launch scheduled on November 14, about four months after Apollo 11 and about a week before the return of the Apollo 11 crew from their world trip.

Chapter Twelve

THE SECOND MOON LANDING WITH APOLLO 12

A pollo 12 was an all Navy crew commanded by Charles (Pete) Conrad, with Dick Gordon and Alan Bean as the command and lunar module pilots respectively. Pete and Gordon had flown a previous Gemini mission together, but it would be a first flight for Bean.

The three were close friends, a bond they developed as naval aviators before joining the space program. The crew's patch was a reflection of their Navy backgrounds as were the space ship names: *Yankee Clipper* for the command module and the *Intrepid* for the lunar landing vehicle.

We learned early on that President and Mrs. Nixon would be attending the launch, a first for a sitting President to attend a manned launch. Former President Lyndon Johnson had been Nixon's guest when Apollo 11 lifted off on July 20.

The President's plane and other charter aircraft landed at the skid strip on the Cape Canaveral Air Force Station the morning of the launch, and guests were transported to the special guest view site. A crowd of about 3,000, far less than the 12,000 who watched Apollo 11 four months earlier, braved cold temperatures and a steady rain.

But the countdown continued and the Saturn V lifted off on schedule before a cheering crowd was stunned when lightning appeared to strike the launch vehicle twice. Liftoff continued and it was learned that the strike caused only minor damage and the mission continued on schedule.

Because of the incident, NASA reviewed weather related issues and changes were made for all future manned and unmanned launches.

A number of things were accomplished during the mission. Commander Pete Conrad piloted *Intrepid* to a perfect landing in the Sea of Storms region of the Moon; but more importantly was able to land within walking distance of the unmanned Surveyor 3 spacecraft, successfully launched by NASA's JPL facility in 1967. Dick Gordon was able to confirm the feat from the orbiting *Yankee Clipper* command module.

Conrad will also be remembered for his remarks as he stepped from the lunar module "Whoopee! Man, that may have been a small step for Neil, but that's a long one for me."

Conrad was followed by Bean, who mistakenly pointed the color camera he was carrying directly into the Sun, which damaged the lens and required the remainder of the surface activity to be filmed in black and white. Nevertheless, Bean became the fourth American to set foot on the Moon.

During the hours spent on the lunar surface, Conrad and Bean collected lunar rocks and soil, but it was their trek to the Surveyor 3 Spacecraft that is most remembered. There they took photographs and retrieved about ten pieces from Surveyor, including the TV camera. All but one of the returned pieces was given to the National Air and Space Museum in Washington, where they are on permanent display.

The mission concluded with *Yankee Clipper* splashing down in the Pacific Ocean on November 24, where the recovery ship USS *Hornet* was waiting like it was four months earlier for the Apollo 11 astronauts. It was an almost perfect landing, but a 16mm film camera dislodged from storage and struck Bean in the forehead. He suffered a mild concussion and the wound required six stitches.

Like the Apollo 11 crew before them, Conrad and his crew were confined to the Mobile Quarantine Facility (MQF) where they received a congratulatory phone call from President Nixon. Splashdown occurred just three days before Thanksgiving, so the crew spent Thanksgiving Day in the MQF where they were served a full turkey dinner.

The quarantine procedure was followed for one additional mission (Apollo 14), but by then it was determined that the Moon was sterile and there was no danger of bringing back space germs so the quarantine procedure was cancelled for the remaining Apollo 15, 16 and 17 missions.

Meanwhile, the plane carrying the Apollo 11 astronauts had already returned from their world trip landing at Andrews Air Force Base on November 5. Helicopters flew the astronauts and their wives to the White House where they were welcomed home by the President and Mrs. Nixon, the Marine Band and a number of dignitaries.

"Giantstep" was not quite finished, because about a month after their return, the astronauts traveled to Ottawa and Montreal in Canada, stops that couldn't fit into the beginning or the completion of the world trip.

After thanking the astronauts for their service as goodwill ambassador on his behalf, he invited them to dinner and to spend the night in the White House. After almost six weeks of attending formal dinners and receptions, the astronauts were able to relax and enjoy dinner with just the President and Mrs. Nixon.

The subject of future plans was raised by the President. He acknowledged that Collins and Secretary of State Rogers had discussed a role in public affairs, not involving media relations but to work as a goodwill ambassador at the State Department.

Armstrong told the President that he hadn't given the matter much thought, but he would probably continue with NASA in whatever position they thought best for him.

Aldrin felt his efforts would best be served in the technical area. He was a graduate of MIT and much of his studies were devoted to orbital mechanics, which NASA used during rendezvous and docking of spacecraft during the Gemini and Apollo program.

After spending the night, the astronauts and wives departed for Andrews Air Force Base and returned to Houston. The three were anxious to receive updates on the progress of the Apollo 12 launch preparations and be of assistance in Mission Control.

All three would leave NASA within three years of their mission. Collins did accept the position of Assistant Secretary of State for Public Affairs, but left after a brief stay to become Director of the Smithsonian's National Air and Space Museum (NASM). It was there he guided the construction phases of the new facility under budget and ahead of schedule where it has become the post popular museum in the world.

Collins is also remembered for writing "Carrying the Fire: An Astronaut's Journey," what is considered by many to be the best book written by a former astronaut. Charles Lindbergh wrote the forward and the book was dedicated to his wife Patrica (Pat), who died in 2014. She was a class gracious Irish lady (Finnegan) who conducted herself with charm wit and dignity.

Mike was the author of other space-related books, but later directed his many talents to water color painting, mostly related to the water and landscape near his Florida Everglades home. Peg and I were fortunate to visit he and Pat at their home on San Marco Island in 1995 and invited to spend the night.

We keep in touch with Mike, especially during the Christmas season. We last saw them both at a "Salute to the Pioneers of Space" event held at the National Naval Aviation Museum in Pensacola, Florida the weekend of December 14-15, 2012.

What probably started during his many public appearances, including the demands of the overseas trip, Aldrin began to have severe cases of depression and alcoholism, which were affecting his career and personal life. His experiences are described in a book "Return to Earth", which he wrote with the help of Los Angles journalist Wayne Warga in 1973.

Aldrin remained with NASA until June 1971, when he decided to return to the Air Force and was assigned an administrative position at Edwards Air Force Base in California before his retirement as a full colonel in March 1972. He and his wife Joan later divorced.

While the Apollo 11 crew was in the final stops on their worldwide tour, we were already involved with early public appearance planning for the Apollo 12 crew. President Nixon had already announced that he planned to send the astronauts and their wives on an overseas trip much like the one by the first lunar landing crew but to different countries.

It was about the same time that Armstrong resigned as an astronaut and accepted an administrative position in the NASA Aeronautics Office in Washington. It was an opportunity to further his research into implementing computer use for high performance aircraft, or more commonly known as "fly by wire." Before arriving in Washington, he had joined Bob Hope's group entertaining troops in Vietnam.

While the program office provided him with secretarial support, Scheer recognized that he would need public affairs assistance. Geneva Barnes was assigned to handle his correspondence, media requests would be handled by Dave Garrett, the PAO for the Office of Space Flight, and I would be the primary contact for his public appearance requests.

The three of us worked as a team and while most matters could be resolved by phone, we often met with Neil, usually after normal work hours. He was almost always available to review media and public requests. His secretary would often phone, asking that I return a call on his behalf. One call I remember was from Armstrong Carpet and Flooring. Even without asking, I kindly rejected their offer for Neil to endorse their products.

Many appearance requests were easily declined, but those considered important or of personal interest to him were discussed and dealt with accordingly.

We were soon receiving written requests from schools all over the country asking for permission to name schools in his honor. Each was discussed personally and he almost always agreed, but I recall his rejection of one of my early acceptance draft letters, which started, "I am honored to accept your request, etc." The suggested letter was returned with a note that he was not honored and there must be someone there more worthy of the honor. So we changed the wording in the acceptance letters to read:

"To the students and faculty: There is no nobler quest than the search for knowledge; for it is knowledge that is the basis for human progress and advancement both on earth and in space. Knowledge gives substance to dreams and brings them to reality. It is knowledge that enabled us to achieve our goal of reaching the moon — long the symbol of the impossible dream. Apollo taught us there are no impossible dreams, that the human will and spirit are indomitable.

"There are unfulfilled goals higher than the moon that have yet to be reached. Among these is the quest for peace, one that has thus far eluded us. Those who spend time within these walls in the pursuit of learning may yet acquire the knowledge and understanding to realize that goal.

"In giving this building of learning my name, you have paid me special honor for which I am most sincerely grateful. However, in doing so, you honor not a man—but Man, and not entirely for what he is but also for what he may become."

By the time he left NASA in 1971, more than twenty schools had been named in his honor.

I felt it fitting that each school should receive a mounted 16x20 color print of Armstrong in his space suit. He agreed to inscribe and sign each photo, but only after assurances that they had requested the photos and we weren't doing it as a matter of practice.

Chapter Thirteen

"Houston, We Have a Problem"

D iscussions between NASA, Department of State and the U.S. Information Agency were underway for the Apollo 12 crew's overseas trip. Meanwhile, we were planning a series of domestic appearances before their departure.

The first I discussed by phone with Conrad while he and the crew was in the MQF. It was an invitation for the crew to appear as Grand Marshalls in the Rose Bowl Parade on New Year's Day in Pasadena, California on January 1, 1970.

Pete also asked about scheduling a visit the NASA Jet Propulsion Laboratory (JPL) in nearby Pasadena the following day, and asked that we accept an invitation extended by the NFL to be honored guests at the Super Bowl in New Orleans on January 11.

Stretch Flanagan and I began working out the details with Rose Bowl officials by phone and we departed for Pasadena two days after Christmas and were on the ground to welcome Pete Conrad, Dick Gordon and Alan Bean when they arrived with their wives aboard the NASA 2 Gulfstream on December 30.

On New Year's Day thousands lined the streets of Pasadena as Conrad in the lead car, followed by Gordon and Bean as they wended their way down the traditional parade route ending at the Rose Bowl luncheon where they were introduced and each spoke. Following the luncheon, the astronauts were introduced and cheered by an estimated 102,000 fans prior to the kickoff to the fifty-sixth Rose Bowl game won by the Southern California Trojans over the University of Michigan Wolverines.

On January 2, the astronauts visited nearby JPL to thank the workers who had contributed so much to not just Apollo, but had been instrumental in many lunar and planetary missions including the successful landing of the Surveyor 3 spacecraft in 1967.

In fact, the Apollo 12 landing site had been chosen with the hope that the Conrad and Bean would be able to walk to Surveyor. The highlight of the JPL visit was the presentation of a piece of the Surveyor Conrad had removed and brought back to present to JPL's director, Bill Pickering.

Before departing for Super Bowl IV in New Orleans, the crew flew to Seattle, Washington, where they were hosted at a civic dinner sponsored by the Pacific Science Center, followed by a thank you visit to the Boeing facilities, the company responsible for development of the Saturn V first stage booster.

After a few days of rest, the crew and their wives flew to New Orleans where they participated in pre-game and halftime activities connected with the fourth and final AFL-NFL World Championship Game (later renamed Super Bowl). The underdog Kansas City Chiefs beat the Minnesota Vikings 23-7.

Like the crew's earlier visit to NASA facilities near Pasadena, it was decided to include thank you stops at nearby Michoud and the Mississippi Test Facility. Both were operated by the Marshall Space Flight Center in Huntsville, Alabama, and were instrumental in the design, construction and testing of the Saturn V rocket engines.

With the success of these thank you appearances, it became standard operating procedure for us to schedule returning astronaut crews to visit and thank workers at contractor facilities in Downey and El Segundo, California, Boeing in Seattle, Bethpage, Long Island and many other space sub contractors located around the country.

It was with the help of these contractors that we were able to expand schedules to include community activities, including school visits and other public functions. These combined efforts helped recognize overall contributions to the space program.

It was now early February and with the Apollo 12 crew overseas, we began to plan for Apollo 13, the seventh manned mission in the Apollo program and the third in the lunar landing program scheduled for launch on April 11, 1970.

The mission would be commanded by veteran astronaut Jim Lovell, who had flown on Gemini, but more recently on Apollo 8. He would be joined by two of the 19 astronauts selected by NASA in 1966, Fred Haise as the lunar module pilot and T.K. (Ken) Mattingly as the command module pilot.

Jack Swigert, who was serving as a member of the backup crew, was at the launch site to look after astronaut families and their guests. We talked several times daily, and he was a frequent and popular visitor to our guest center.

Rumors had been circulating launch week that Mattingly would be pulled from the flight after it was learned that he had been exposed to the German Measles. While Lovell argued to retain him, he finally accepted Swigert as a replacement.

Seventy-two hours before the launch, Swigert called me to say he would no longer be involved with guest operations and had just been assigned to replace Ken Mattingly as the command module pilot. Needless to say, I was in a state of shock. One moment he was working with me, and in a day or two would be making his first space flight and not even he would have guessed the outcome.

Shortly after the launch, Jack realized he would be in space and not able to complete work on his income taxes by the April 15 filing date. NASA contacted the IRS and was able to obtain a filing extension. Under the circumstances, I don't believe he paid a penalty.

Apollo 13 lifted off on April 11, and Lovell became the first man to fly to the Moon twice. Fifty-five hours into the flight an explosion occurred in one of the service module's oxygen tanks, prompting Commander Jim Lovell's now famous response, "Houston, we've got a problem," and the beginning of a long and intense interaction with the astronauts and the flight controllers in Mission Control.

The astronauts were able to evacuate the damaged *Odyssey* command and service module and move into the Lunar Module *Aquarius*, which they used as effective lifeboat until they were able to reenter just before splashdown.

In his book "Lost Moon", which Ron Howard made into an Academy Award-nominated movie "Apollo 13" starring Tom Hanks, Lovell believes teamwork and the ingenuity of the people in Mission Control assured the return of the crippled spacecraft to Earth and a mission often referred to as the successful failure, which came to a conclusion when *Odyssey* splashed down in the South Pacific on April 17, 1970, with all three astronauts safely back on Earth.

President Nixon had been informed of the explosion by National Security Advisor Henry Kissinger and Chief of Staff H.R. Haldeman. Administrator Thomas Paine confirmed that one of the two oxygen tanks aboard the command module had exploded, causing a catastrophic mechanical failure that ruled out the possibility of continuing with a lunar landing, and that the crew was working with Mission Control in what was becoming a life and death drama.

Bill Anders, who had been named executive secretary for the National Aeronautics and Space Council by Vice President Agnew, and remembered for his astronaut role on Apollo 8, became the primary liaison for the President and his staff. Briefings based on conversations between Mission Control and the astronauts were held in a White House Situation Room.

Anders reported that the crew was tired but generally in good shape and spirits and it was beginning to look like Apollo 13 would be limping home safely.

Anders was joined by fellow astronaut Michael Collins as they briefed the President and Kissinger watching on TV for parachute deployment and confirmation of splashdown, which occurred at 1:08 pm on April 17, 142 hours 54 minutes and 41 seconds after launch.

At the same time in Mission Control, Flight Controller Gerry Griffin flashes a triumphant thumbs up, and is joined by fellow controllers Gene (failure is not an option) Kranz and Glynn Lunney.

The President placed a call to the USS *Iwo Jima*, the carrier recovery ship, and spoke briefly with the crew and then delivered a statement to the nation. The following day he and the first lady departed on Air Force One for Houston to award the Presidential Medal of Freedom to the Apollo 13 mission operations team, acknowledging the crucial role the ground team played in bringing the crew back home safely.

He and the First Lady, accompanied by the astronaut spouses and Swigert's parents, then flew to Hawaii to award the three astronauts with the nation's highest civilian honor. His presentation remarks included a reference to not reaching the moon but reaching the hearts of millions of people on earth by what they did.

Expecting the worst but hoping for a miracle, The White House staff had prepared a contingency plan in the event of a disaster. Frank Borman, who was already known and respected by the Administration, became involved with White House aide Dwight Chapin.

The two discussed options that were conveyed in a memorandum from Chapin to Haldeman. That memo was classified at the time, but the author had no problem obtaining a copy from the President Nixon Foundation and Museum.

Meanwhile, we were back in Washington sorting through the hundreds of letters and communications from around the world, many requesting appearances by the crew. We learned from the White House that the President was considering sending the astronauts on a good will mission abroad.

Following the return to Houston and the debriefings to determine what caused the oxygen tank explosion, the astronauts posed for a new crew picture and were free to begin a series of appearances in the U.S. As expected, both the cities of New York and Chicago were in with their usual requests.

Chicago's was unique because, not only did they want to honor the three astronauts, but also the flight crew members in Mission Control for their around the clock work to save the crew and get the three astronauts around the Moon and back to Earth before their life-supporting consumables ran out.

The astronauts and the team in mission control were a testament to the preparation, skill and resourcefulness that ensured survival in space and the safe return.

Following the triumphant return to Houston and a series of debriefings before NASA officials, the astronauts were prepared to share their experiences with a worldwide audience beginning with a press conference.

I was in almost daily contact by phone with Lovell to discuss countless requests for appearances. We quickly agreed to the Chicago and New York requests, as well as a visit to Washington for a White House welcome and Capital Hill receptions.

Mayor Daley greeted the astronauts and flight controllers on their arrival, and the city of Chicago welcomed the crew and flight controllers in a ticker tape parade around the loop and at a civic luncheon at the Palmer House, where Honorary Citizenship Awards were presented to Swigert and Haise, who suffered a urinary tract infection during the mission and did not make the Chicago trip.

Lovell, who had received the award after Apollo 8, was instead awarded the City of Chicago's Medal of Merit. The flight controllers honored were Siguard Sjoberg, Milt Windler, Gene Kranz, Gerry Griffin and Glynn Lunney.

Following the lunch, Lovell and Swigert were driven to Orchestra Hall, where a questions and answer session had been arranged before 2,500 high school students. Questions had been written and submitted in advance and, because of time restraints, many went unanswered.

On the NASA plane to Washington, I recall Lovell thumbing through some of the unanswered questions, shaking his head, when he came to one asking, "Where does space end and infinity begin?"

"Boy, I am sure glad I didn't have to answer that one," he said.

During the flight, Lovell and I had time to review a speech he was scheduled to deliver that evening to a group of POW/MIA families at Constitution Hall. While he had prepared remarks, we were able to review the speech and made necessary changes.

He wanted the families to know that while the Navy had assigned him to NASA, as an astronaut, he was first a U.S. Naval Aviator sharing concern for the welfare of their loved ones being held prisoner in Vietnam. He received a warm welcome, and after his closing remarks took the time to meet and talk with many wives and family members.

During the crew's Washington visit and a series of meetings with NASA and congressional officials, Scheer had arranged with Lovell for the astronauts to visit Hickory Hill, a stately white brick mansion on six acres in the McLean area of Virginia, once owned by forebears of Confederate General Robert E. Lee.

It was purchased in the 1950's by then-Senator John F. Kennedy, who later sold it to his brother Robert and wife Ethel. She continued to live there following the assassination of her husband two years earlier.

As the group departed, they left knowing they had been able to see and learn the important role Hickory Hill had played throughout American history. It was sold by Mrs. Kennedy in 2009.

Ceremonies in New York were arranged by Bud Palmer, Chief of Protocol for Mayor John Lindsay. The event included a presentation of medals, keys to the city, a civic luncheon and visit to the United Nations.

Three social events were added while the astronauts were in New York. Mayor and Mrs. John Lindsay hosted the group to a showing of the Broadway show "Company", starring Lauren Bacall, which was followed by a celebrity party at the famous Sardi's Restaurant in the Theater District of Manhattan. The guest list included Danny Kaye,

Richard Rodgers, Ethel Merman, Eli Wallach, Johnny Carson, Pearl Bailey, Skitch Henderson and other Broadway and Hollywood stars.

Haise, still suffering from the effects of the kidney infection, decided to skip the last social event and return to Houston, while The Lovells and Swigert, who was a confirmed bachelor, had agreed to attend a showing of the controversial Broadway show "Hair", a rock musical including profanity, use of illegal drugs and irreverence for the American flag. Lovell felt that attending would be an acknowledgment of the life-saving role their lunar module "Aquarius" (a popular song in the show) had played in their historical mission.

The show was especially controversial because of its anti-war theme and opposition to the Vietnam War that was also prevalent in many cities and college campuses. To be sure, we brought the matter to the attention of Scheer and to get NASA's reaction. He agreed that, while controversial, he had no problem with our decision to attend.

I confirmed the appearance with Mrs. Michael Gifford, a "Hair" representative, and we arranged for the Lovells and friends to be seated in the mezzanine, while I sat with Swigert in the Biltmore Theater's orchestra pit.

It was apparent during the first act that the astronauts were displeased with the performance and what they felt to be slurs directed towards the American flag. At the intermission, Swigert was the first to leave and we headed for the exit and hailed a taxicab. The Lovells followed, leaving me to talk to Mrs. Gifford and explain the early departures.

A reporter asked Swigert why they were leaving and he responded, "I don't like what you are doing to the flag; I don't like the way they wrapped the flag around that guy." In that scene, three characters are onstage with an American flag and one of them wraps himself in it.

I apologized to Mrs. Gifford, saying our walkout was no reflection on the show or the cast, but the American flag was a symbol of the country that overcame great odds to return them safely to Earth just a few weeks earlier and they felt it was being disrespected. She felt our departure was premature and that had we waited we would have heard the line in the show saying the American flag was "the best one yet."

News of the walkout appeared in the next day edition of the *New York Times* and other newspapers complete with pictures, but memories of the event soon faded from memory as the war in Vietnam continued to dominate the news.

Of the many experiences associated with my job, I have to consider my involvement with these three astronauts between April and the fall of 1970 as the most demanding, yet most satisfying, in my NASA career up to that time.

Following the New York trip, I supported Swigert for a week of hometown appearances in Denver, Colorado, including a commencement speech he delivered at his alma mater, the University of Colorado in Boulder. Tom Brookshire, a CBS NFL broadcaster of NFL games at the time, introduced Jack and recalled that they had played together for the Golden Buffalos years earlier,

My relationship with Jack was such that he invited me to move from a nearby hotel into the home of his parents, Dr. and Mrs. Leonard Swigert, where I continued to coordinate and staff his many other appearances. I always felt close to Jack, and that friendship continued during the years even after he left NASA in April 1973 to become Executive Director of the Committee on Science and Technology in the U.S. House of Representatives and its chairman, Olin Teague of Texas.

Back in Washington, I began working with Scheer and St. Clair to plan the first year commemoration of Apollo 11. It would be a one-day event on July 20, 1970, and would include stops by Armstrong, Collins and Aldrin in Jefferson City, Missouri, the United Nations in New York City and conclude with a dinner back in Washington D.C.

The three astronauts, Administrator Paine, Scheer, St. Clair, Bill Taub and me, departed Andrews Air Force Base in a Learjet early the morning of July 20, for the flight to Jefferson City , Missouri. The Missouri Capitol was chosen because it was a chance for the astronauts to be re-united with *Columbia*, the Apollo 11 command module that took them to the moon and was now part of a traveling flatbed trailer exhibit to all fifty state capitals, and just happened to be there on the anniversary day.

Following completion of the two-year, fifty states tour, *Columbia* went on permanent display in the Smithsonian Arts and Industries Building before moving to the National Air and Space Museum when it opened in 1976.

Following opening remarks by Missouri Governor Warren Hearnes, the three astronauts made brief remarks and departed for New York City and a drive to the United Nations, where they were introduced and presented UN Secretary General U Thant with an Apollo lunar rock.

The anniversary day concluded with a small informal dinner hosted by Administrator Paine at the Hay Adams Hotel back in Washington. While this was the first, anniversaries were held to commemorate Apollo 11 every fifth year. I was involved with planning those in 1974, 1979, 1984 and the 20th in 1989. I retired in May 1994, about the time planning was well underway to celebrate the 25th anniversary. In 2019 we will celebrate the 50th anniversary of Apollo 11.

The observance plans for each were first discussed with Armstrong followed by concurrences from Collins and Aldrin. To them he was, and still remained, mission commander, and they would follow his lead. Armstrong always questioned why NASA wanted to observe July 20 every fifth year.

He always insisted that all crews and current and former astronauts be included, emphasizing his desire that the observance focus on the accomplishments of the Apollo program and not just his crew. While many former and current astronauts participated and were acknowledged and introduced, the media's focus was always on Apollo 11 and the crew.

The NASA public affairs media office in Washington always prepared an anniversary press kit featuring updated crew biographies and a summary of the historic mission, and was available to members of the media so that they could write articles and produce radio and TV programs in advance of the observances.

The first anniversary in 1970 was a one-day affair, but the July 1974 observance was expanded to include several days beginning with a news conference in Washington and a flight to the Kennedy Space Center on July 16, five years to the day and time of their launch and to participate in the dedication of their launch pad 39-A, which had been declared a National Landmark by the U.S. Park Service.

Following introductions and brief remarks, they listened to a recording of the last moments of commentator Jack King's countdown five years earlier. "3,2,1, we have liftoff, at exactly 9:32 a.m. The three then lifted a red, white and blue-striped banner unveiling of the National Landmark plaque.

The observance continued in Washington July 21, when the three astronauts and Administrator Dr. T.O. Paine joined in a ceremony at the National Cathedral and the presentation of a small 7.18 gram basalt lunar rock from the Sea of Tranquility. The rock was donated by Paine for the centerpiece of a Space Window, symbolizing both spiritual and scientific connections to the mystery of the cosmos, and has since become one of best-loved stained glass windows in the Cathedral.

The 1979 tenth anniversary would be the first of all future anniversary events held at the National Air and Space Museum (NASM), which had opened on July 1, 1976 for the U.S. Bi-Centennial. It was a natural venue and provided a perfect setting with historic airplanes and spacecraft.

Also, who better to be there than Mike Collins and *Columbia*, the Command Module he had piloted on that historic mission now sitting as the centerpiece in the lobby of the museum.

Most observances began with a photo opportunity with the crew around the *Columbia* spacecraft, usually followed by a series of interviews conducted by the hosts of the network morning TV shows in front of the full-scale replica of the Lunar Module *Eagle*.

The crew then made visits to Capitol Hill, where they met with Senate and House leaders and members of the space committees. During this observance, the commanders of the first two lunar landings were accompanied by Terry Finn, NASA's director of congressional relations, with Pete Conrad and the author with Armstrong.

The day usually concluded the evening of July 20, with a NASM reception for all astronauts, NASA headquarters and field center representatives, contractors and individuals cited for their roles in the success of Apollo 11 and succeeding missions.

It was mid-summer of 1970 when I accompanied Armstrong to West Germany, where he was the honored guest at the dedication of a glider museum August 8-9 at Wasserkuppe, the birthplace of glider flying and famous for its optimum air currents in the Rhon Mountains. He also used the occasion to visit West German aircraft facilitates in Munich.

I have two distinctive memories of the dedication and the soaring events. The first was when Neil introduced me to Hanna Reitsch, the world-famous German aviatrix test pilot and the only woman awarded the Iron Cross, who had set over 40 altitude and endurance women's records in gliding.

Neil had enjoyed the friendly, but secure, surroundings that weekend, but our Sunday morning departure was not without incident. As we prepared to depart by automobile, security was unable to control the crowds of autograph-seeking people. Event sponsors were able to move our vehicle to the rear kitchen entrance where the crowds were distracted long enough for us to depart for Munich.

The U.S. Consulate in Munich coordinated our transportation and hotel arrangements and had prepared a one-day schedule for Neil to tour numerous aircraft plants on Monday, August 11, including a stop at the famous Messerschmitt facility, where he was able to fly an experimental helicopter.

As we prepared to return to Washington, I was informed by St. Clair to remain in Germany and provide public affairs support for the Apollo 14 crew (Alan Shepard, Edgar Mitchell, Gene Cernan and Joe Engle), who were in nearby Nordlingen, Bavaria, conducting geology experiments in preparation for their flight in early 1971.

The site was chosen because it sits near the impact point of a meteorite that struck the Earth around 15 million years ago. The soil and rock formations were similar to what the astronauts expected to find at their Fra Mauro lunar landing site.

My job was to accompany the astronauts to and from the geology site and to control members of the German press who were interested in obtaining interviews. Shepard and I determined there would be no interviews, but agreed to a press conference at the conclusion of the field trip.

I moderated the question and answer session with the help of a U.S. Information Agency representative. It was finally time to fly home and I arrived at Dulles, tired, but none the worse for the experience.

It was now mid-August and I was looking forward to some family vacation time before beginning preparations for the Apollo 14 launch in January. The Apollo 13 accident review board was nearing completion of its investigation into the oxygen tank explosion and had determined proposed fixes would prevent a reoccurrence.

Meanwhile, NASA, the White House and the State Department were in serious discussions regarding an overseas goodwill trip by the Apollo 13 astronauts. The life and death experience of the crew had generated worldwide interest, especially in countries not previously visited by the first two lunar-landing crews.

A staff to support the trip (appropriately named "Aquarius") was headed by Tom Mosselum, a veteran U.S. State Department executive, with my boss Wade St. Clair, his deputy. Others included Bill Taub, the NASA photographer, Bill O'Donnell, a public affairs officer, to help with preparation of speeches and Mary Lou Hendrickson, Julian Scheer's secretary, who would provide secretarial support. NASA was able to obtain a C-135 aircraft and an Air Force crew from Special Air Missions at Andrews Air Force Base for the trip.

An approved itinerary called for the trip to begin on October 1 and conclude two weeks later with stops in Iceland, Switzerland, Greece (a rest stop in Crete), a trip to Malta, and conclude with a train ride through the Republic of Ireland.

Just prior to the start of the trip, St. Clair informed me that I had been added to the traveling staff and would be the "gifts and presentations" officer. This would require the preparation of appropriate gifts the crew would present to heads of state, other dignitaries, and museums.

The trip was ready to begin and the astronaut party departed Andrews Air Force Base for Reykjavik, the capital of Iceland, on October 1. The arrival was set to coincide with the opening of the country's opera season that night and the astronauts were to be introduced as honored guests.

We arrived at the U.S Naval Station at Keflavik outside Reykjavik late that afternoon, leaving the astronauts and their wives very little time to prepare for the concert. I recall Lovell telling me of a knock on his door while getting dressed for the concert, opening to find Swigert, who asked if Marilyn could sew a button on his sport coat.

Jack was not only known for his bachelor status, but for his frugality. Kenny Mohr, who was a member of our crew flight staff responsible for baggage handling, related to me his dismay that Swigert began our trip with one garment bag. Lovell handed Mohr money and instructed him to buy two suits for Swigert at our next stop.

The concert and appearances the next day went as planned and a highlight of the visit was a tour. Iceland, which became a republic in 1944, is famous for its dramatic volcanic landscape of geysers, hot springs, glaciers and black-sand beaches. The majority of the population relies on geothermal power.

It was soon goodbye to our newly made friends in Iceland, and our aircraft was headed to Switzerland and a series of appearances in Zurich, Bern and Lucerne. While there, arrangements had been made for the three astronauts to travel to Lake Constance, West Germany, for the 21st Astronautical Congress.

There they were joined by fellow astronaut James McDivitt, who gave a technical account of the Apollo 13 oxygen explosion. Three Soviet cosmonauts attended to demonstrate the cooperative space spirit of the two nations. The crew's presentation resembled a news conference, with film highlights of their mission and the cosmonauts participated. Lovell and one of the cosmonauts exchanged space pins.

While the trip to Switzerland included stops in Zurich and Bern, the primary event was an appearance by the three astronauts at the Swiss Museum of Transport, Switzerland's most popular museum in Lucerne, which opened in 1959 and features the development of traffic on roads, rail, water in the air and space.

Following a two-day stop in Athens, Greece, where the astronauts called on numerous government officials and made presentations, it was on to the Greek island of Crete for a weekend rest stop. Of course the trip to Athens included a tour of the Acropolis, the ancient citadel containing the remains of several ancient buildings including the Parthenon and other symbols of Greek civilization.

The next to final stop on the trip was a stop in Valletta, the capital of Malta, an archipelago in the central Mediterranean, between Sicily and the North African coast with a history of colonial control spanning centuries. Independence was achieved from Britain in 1964. It was during the flight that I celebrated my 35th birthday, complete with a cake and an autographed photo inscribed by Haise.

While it was an official visit, the astronauts enjoyed the leisure schedule and the cheering crowds that gathered for their every move in an antique Rolls Royce limousine convertible. They were especially appreciative of the thousands of school children dressed in parochial school uniforms who lined the narrow streets, and people cheering from balconies and waving American flags.

Our final stop was to the Republic of Ireland, which would be remembered for a number of unforgettable experiences. The first was the welcome by Ireland's President, Eamon de Valera, on his birthday. De Valera was one of the most important figures in the history of Ireland.

The second was the Limerick Music Train, a unique journey aboard an antique train that afforded us a look at the greenest countryside in the world, reminding the astronauts that they had indeed returned to the cool green hills of Earth.

Our Irish hosts had arranged for our group to experience a medieval banquet (luncheon) at the 15th century Bunratty Castle. As we arrived and crossed over a drawbridge and ascended the castle steps, a kilted piper played a tune of welcome.

We then entered the Great Hall, resplendent with 16th century furniture and tapestries, and were served a goblet of Mead while mingling with the Ladies of the Castle, as a medieval Madrigal related the Castle's history. It was then that Captain and Mrs. Lovell were ceremoniously crowned Earl and Lady before moving to the Great Banquet Hall and candle lit bench seating, reminiscent of the medieval period.

An Irish harp and fiddle provided entertainment while the party enjoyed a four-course dinner and fine wines on the long oak tables. In keeping with the tradition of the event, the butler revealed a scoundrel (Jack Swigert) and the Earl had to decide his fate. For Jack, the punishment was to escort two lovely Irish lassies, and the group roared its approval.

Before leaving, Lovell thanked our hosts and handed out signed Apollo 13 presentation items. We then departed for another castle (Dromoland), originally the ancestral home of one of the few families of Gaelic Royalty, where arrangements had been made for us to spend the night.

We were not disappointed in the accommodations. Stately guest rooms featured crystal chandeliers, and antique furnishings that combined history and convenience. For dinner, we ordered off the menu, where our meals featured an Irish twist.

The following morning we departed for home from nearby Shannon International Airport marking the end of a memorable two-week goodwill mission on behalf of the President of the United States.

Chapter Fourteen

BACK TO THE MOON WITH APOLLO 14

W ork on the scheduled Apollo 14 was well underway when I returned. This would be the first Apollo launch since the conclusion of the investigation into the cause of the Apollo 13 accident. The Apollo 14 spacecraft, named *Kitty Hawk*, had undergone modifications designed to prevent the possibility of another explosion in space.

Public interest had been building since this would be the first launch since the accident, but the media focused on Shepard, who had been grounded since 1963 because of an inner ear disease.

While disappointed, he had remained with NASA and was named chief of the astronaut office. In 1968 he underwent a successful operation in which a small drain tube was implanted in his inner ear.

His application for readmission was approved after much lobbying, and his patience and determination was rewarded when NASA chose him to command Apollo 14. He was quoted as saying, "I think if a person wants something badly enough, he's just got to hang in there and keep at it." At age 47, he was the oldest astronaut in the program to fly in space, until that distinction would belong to John Glenn, when he flew as a Mission Specialist on the Space Shuttle in 1998 at the age of 77.

Liftoff occurred on January 31, 1971, nearly ten years after his historic first space flight, and will be remembered for a problem command module pilot Stu Roosa experienced in the docking of the two spacecrafts and the first use of a lunar cart Shepard and lunar module pilot Ed Mitchell brought with them to help during two trips outside the spacecraft.

An added twist and a surprise to almost everyone was when Shepard, an avid golfer back home, became the first person to hit a golf ball on the Moon. In fact, he hit two with a lunar tool that had been modified with the head of a six iron by a Houston golf pro.

After the flight, my office began receiving phone calls and letters requesting more information about the shots. I placed a phone call to

Al, and he was eager to set the record straight. After all these years I still have the typewritten notes from our conversation.

"I used a contingency sample handle with a six iron head. It was a four-section aluminum handle that telescoped together and was assembled by an anonymous professional at the River Oaks Country Club near Houston.

I hit two shots and the first was the best, carrying about 200 yards. I shanked the second because I could not pivot or get any arm length at all because of the space suit, and the ball did not travel any appreciable distance."

Since the makeshift club was the property of the U.S Government, in 1973 Shepard requested, and was granted permission, to present the club to the U.S. Golf Association Museum at Far Hills, New Jersey. A replica is on permanent display in the Air and Space Museum in Washington.

Meanwhile, administrative changes were taking place at NASA Headquarters. Dr. T.O. Paine, who became Acting Administrator after the departure of Webb in 1969 and was later appointed Administrator by Nixon in 1970, resigned.

His deputy, Dr. George M. Low, was named Acting Administrator and served until the appointment of Dr. James C. Fletcher. It was during the interim in March that Low fired Scheer, who had enjoyed a remarkable relationship beginning with Webb and continued under Paine.

Some members of Congress had lodged complaints about Scheer but were unable to get Webb or Paine to fire him, but were successful during Low's brief time in an acting capacity. Days later, the *Washington Post* published an editorial questioning Scheer's firing, citing NASA's public affairs program as one of government's finest.

Dr. James C. Fletcher, former President of the University of Utah, became NASA's fourth administrator about a month later. Fletcher left NASA in 1977 after the election of President Jimmy Carter, but was appointed the seventh NASA Administrator by President Reagan in 1986.

Scheer left a lasting public affairs legacy that has never been matched. He received the agency's highest honor, The Distinguished Service Medal, after Apollo 11. He had played a major role in determining the wording on the lunar module plaque that read: "We came in Peace for All Mankind," and suggested the name "Columbia" for the

Apollo 11 command module, but is probably best remembered for his insistence that NASA engineers get a TV camera aboard the landing *Eagle* spacecraft on Apollo 11.

After leaving NASA, he became campaign manager for North Carolina's Terry Sanford's unsuccessful presidential campaign, and served in many corporate positions, while remaining active in environmental issues. He died in a tragic accident at his home in Virginia in September 2001.

With the successful splashdown of *Kitty Hawk* and the return of the Apollo 14 crew to Houston, we were already at work on a schedule of public appearances. Mayor Richard Daley of Chicago and John Lindsay of New York were in with their usual requests for the crew to receive ticker tape receptions and the honors received by previous Apollo crews.

The Air Force at Andrews Air Force Base furnished a C-118 air missions aircraft for the astronauts and their families. The first stop was in Chicago and the ticker tape parade down State Street and a luncheon hosted by Mayor Daley with Jimmy Durante serving as the MC.

It was then on to New York and another parade before a luncheon and visit to the United Nations, where the crew was welcomed by then U.N. Ambassador George H.W. Bush and Secretary General U Thant.

During the three-day stay in "The Big Apple", the astronauts were interviewed on several evening talk shows and guests of ABC's Frank Reynolds and space reporter Jules Bergman on ABC's Sunday's Issues and Answers show.

But the big event on the schedule was an invitation to join Mayor Lindsay and his party at the heavyweight boxing match featuring Muhammad Ali and Smoking Joe Frazier on Monday, March 8, in Madison Square Garden.

It marked the return of Ali to the boxing ring after his reinstatement. He had been stripped of his heavyweight title earlier because of his refusal to register for the military draft. I was fortunate to be there and to see a great fight won by Frasier in a 15 round unanimous decision. It was the first time two undefeated boxers fought each other for the heavyweight crown.

A few weeks later I accompanied Shepard back to New York City for two events. The first was a luncheon at Gallagher's Restaurant in midtown Manhattan, where he was named to the 1971 All America

Invitation from President and Mrs. Richard Nixon for the Apollo 11 state dinner.

President Richard Nixon presents the Apollo 11 astronauts with the Presidential Medals of Freedom, August 13, 1969.

Guests of the Presidential state dinner in honor of the Apollo 11 astronauts were given a commemorative plaque matching the one left on the lunar surface by Neil Armstrong and Buzz Aldrin.

President Lyndon and Lady Bird Johnson watched the liftoff of Apollo 11 at Kennedy Space Center. At the time the facility was named Cape Kennedy, but was later changed to KSC.

This historic picture includes signatures from the Apollo 11 astronauts, President Richard Nixon, and NASA Administrator T.O. Paine.

Neil Armstrong, with sons Mark and Rick, waves to an adoring crowd en route to the Wapakoneta Fairgrounds. The author is pictured in the front passenger seat.

Unveiling of the "First Man on the Moon" stamp, which featured Neil Armstrong stepping onto the lunar service. Both Armstrong and Buzz Aldrin were disappointed that the stamp only recognized Armstrong's achievement.

Neil meets German aviatrix test pilot Hanna Reitsch at the glider museum dedication in Wasserkuppe, Germany, August 1970.

Worn out from months of travel, the author takes a nap while flying to the next big event, 1974.

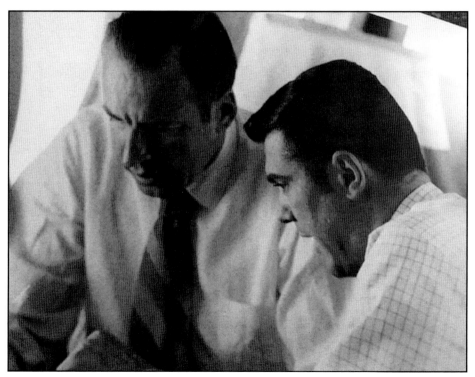

The author and Jim Lovell review a speech he will deliver at a meeting of POW-MIA families at Constitution Hall in Washington, D.C., May 1970.

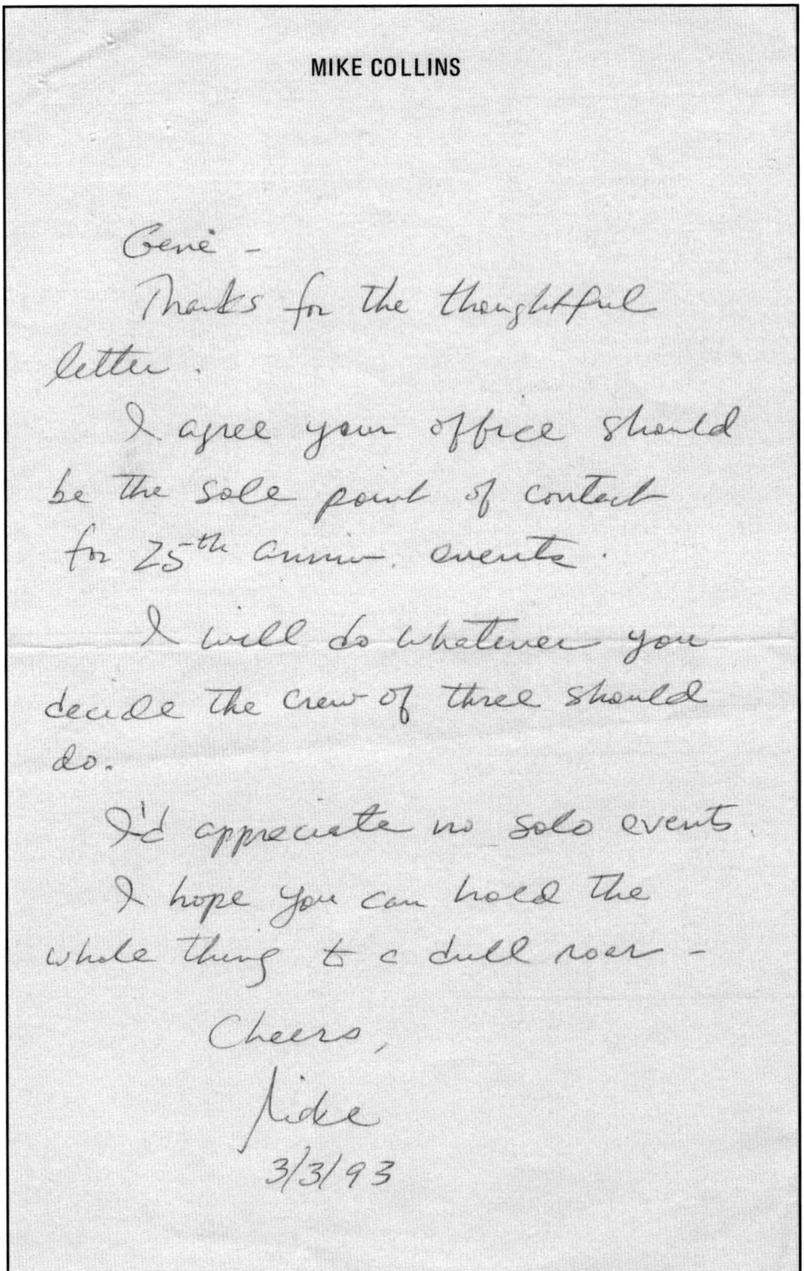

MIKE COLLINS

Gene –

Thanks for the thoughtful letter.

I agree your office should be the sole point of contact for 25th Anniv. events.

I will do whatever you decide the crew of three should do.

I'd appreciate no solo events. I hope you can hold the whole thing to a dull roar –

Cheers,

Mike

3/3/93

Letter from Mike Collins regarding the 25th Anniversary events for Apollo 11, March 3, 1993.

The author's wife, Peg, is flanked by NASA photographer Bill Taub and Astronaut Mike Collins.

Parade honoring Apollo 11 astronauts Armstrong, Collins and Aldrin, August 13, 1969.

Group photo of the Apollo 11 astronauts, their wives, and many members of the "Giant Step" support team, July 19, 1979.

John Lindsay, Mayor of New York City, presents gold medals to the crew of Apollo 11, August 13, 1969.

Astronaut Edwin E. Aldrin Jr. addresses the assemblage at City Hall after presentation of the New York City Medal of Honor by Mayor John Lindsay, August 13, 1969.

Author briefs the wives of Apollo 11 astronauts aboard Air Force One during flight from Chicago to Los Angeles on August 13, 1969. The wives to the author's right are Janet Armstrong, Joan Aldrin, and Pat Collins. They asked questions about the rumored world trip they and their husbands would make on behalf of the President.

Gene Marianetti

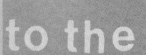

to the

LUNAR MODULE HAS
LANDED ON MOON

It was on May 25, 1961, in an address to Congress, that President John F. Kennedy said: "I believe that this nation should commit itself to achieving the goal, before this decade is out, of landing a man on the moon and returning him safely to earth . . ."

It was on Sunday, July 20, 1969 (at 10:56:20 p.m. EDT), about 6½ hours after Neil A. Armstrong and Edwin E. "Buzz" Aldrin, Jr., landed their spaceship Eagle on the lunar surface, that Armstrong first put foot on the surface of the moon and said: "That's one small step for a man, one giant leap for mankind."

Man's first footfall in a world other than his own, acclaimed the most dramatic moment in the history of mankind, was viewed by a worldwide television audience . . . including at least one Montanan with almost as personal a concern for the safety and success of the astronauts as their families.

Gene Marianetti, former KMON radio (Great Falls) news director and later an intern in the office of Montana Sen. Lee Metcalf, is now chief protocol officer for NASA's astronauts.

Advance and post-launch press and VIP arrangements as well as coordinating speaking and personal appearances of the NASA astronauts rank as among Gene's main areas of responsibility in the U. S. space program.

However, while the job responsibilities may include only the on-earth activities of the astronauts, the picture (upper left) of Gene maintaining a TV vigil during the lunar module descent and moon landing shows that his real concern never ends. Also sharing his prayerful "sweat out" concern during the mission is Gene's wife, Peggy, pictured at the bottom of this page in a nail-biting agony of suspense as the lunar module approached the moon's surface.

Only when the television screen flashed "LUNAR MODULE HAS LANDED ON THE MOON" (picture at right) did the charged tenseness of life in the Marianetti household ease to within tolerable limits.

Nor does the family concern end with Gene and Peggy. While daughter Kelly, 11 months, may be unconcerned at all the fuss, certainly Randy, 14, Michael, 12, and Jamie, 9, the three older Marianetti children, are equally as intensely avid as their parents in following every step of every manned space launch.

As Gene puts it:

"Once you could say 'the sky's the limit' when you wanted to express an ultimate; today the phrase has to be expanded because there seems to be no limit on man's capabilities. Certainly I'm more than proud to be a part of what has to be man's greatest adventure — the exploration of space."

(EDITOR'S NOTE: Thanks to the thoughtful consideration of Dr. Thomas O. Paine, administrator of NASA, and the many courtesies of Gene Marianetti, chief protocol officer for the astronauts, I was included among the 3,000 guests from around the globe invited to attend the July 16 "moon shot" at Cape Kennedy, Fla. The coincidence of being the only rural electric editor at the history-making launch provided the inspiration for this month's center-spread picture story.

Incidentally, the experience of VIP treatment — complete with motorcycle escorts, special briefings and tours, and the thrill of actually witnessing the moon launch — will be a treasured memory always.—Ray W. Fenton, editor of MREN)

Peggy Marianetti

Montanans 'Sweat Out' History

Special feature on the author and the space program in Montana Rural Electric News Magazine, *September 1969.*

Official Apollo 12 patch.

The crew of Apollo 12, l-r: Charles "Pete" Conrad Jr., Richard F. Gordon Jr., and Alan Bean.

Apollo 12 astronaut Alan Bean

Pete Conrad and Alan Bean at the site of the Surveyor 3 spacecraft.

Apollo 13 mission patch

The Apollo 13 astronauts in an updated crew photo after John Swigert replaced T.K. Mattingly prior to the launch.

126

Jack Swigert

Apollo 13 drifts back to Earth after safely travelling to the Moon and back.

Flight Controller Gerry Griffin (far left) flashes a triumphant thumbs up after the crew of Apollo 13 make it back to Earth. To his left are fellow controllers Gene Kranz and Glynn Lunney.

A happy crew of Apollo 13, l-r: Fred Haise, John Swigert, and Jim Lovell.

The author received this unique birthday gift from the team of Apollo 13 in 1970.

Motorcade down Michigan Ave. in Chicago for the crew of Apollo 13, May 1, 1970.

During the Medieval Banquet at Bunratty Castle, Jack Swigert is revealed as a scoundrel and punished to escort these two lovely ladies.

The crew of Apollo 13 attended a Medieval Banquet at Bunratty Castle, County Clare, Ireland. Here the Captain and Mrs. Lovell were ceremoniously crowned Earl and Lady for the event.

The Apollo 13 crew at the Swiss Museum of Transport in Lucerne, Switzerland.

The Apollo 13 crew ride in a vintage Rolls Royce during a motorcade at Valletta, the capital of Malta.

Bill Anders and Mike Collins (seated) at the White House during the Apollo 13 mission.

Ticker tape, confetti and cheers from the crowds greeted Apollo 13 astronauts John Swigert, and James Lovell as they attended the national major civic reception, May 1, 1970.

Apollo 14 mission patch

Alan Shepard's golf swing on the Moon

Apollo 14 crew interviewed by talk show host Joey Bishop, April 1971.

Jimmy Durante served as MC when the Apollo 14 crew visited Chicago in March 1971.

Alan Shepard with author being welcomed to Gallagher's Restaurant in New York City prior to a luncheon during which Shepard was named to the 1971 All-American Golf Team.

Alan Shepard gives his acceptance speech as a member of the 1971 All-American Golf Team, April 1971.

Apollo 14 Motorcade in New York City, March 1971.

The crew of Apollo 14 attended the Ali-Frazier Fight at Madison Square Garden, March 8, 1971.

Apollo 15 mission patch

Apollo 15 astronauts Dave Scott and Al Worden flank Barbara Lawrence, widow of aerospace research pilot and U.S. Air Force Major Robert H. Lawrence Jr., during the crew's welcome to Chicago in 1971. Her 31-year-old husband was killed in the crash of his jet trainer aircraft on December 8, 1967 at Edwards Air Force Base. Had he lived, it is believed he may have become the first African American to fly aboard the Space Shuttle. The author is seen at far left.

The author (left) with Jack "Black Jack" Reilly and Ed Pierce in Chicago.

With the NASA Gulfstream in the background, the author borrowed photographer Bill Taub's camera and took this photo during Apollo 15's visit to New York. Pictured l-r: NASA PAO Bill Lloyd, crew Scott, Irwin, Worden, and Taub.

Pope Paul VI welcomes the author, Apollo 15 astronauts, crewmembers and their wives during a visit to the Vatican, November 17, 1971.

The Apollo 15 crew with New York Mayor John Lindsay during a NYC motorcade.

Apollo 16 mission patch

New York Mayor John Lindsay accepts an Apollo 16 photo from Commander John Young during the crew's visit to New York in June 1972. Young holds hands with wife, Suzy, and to the left of the mayor are crewmates Charlie Duke, wife Dotti, and T.K. Mattingly.

John Young's thank you note to the author, which included a flown U.S. flag and mission patch.

Apollo 17 mission patch

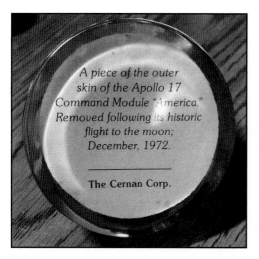

A piece of the outer
skin of the Apollo 17
Command Module "America."
Removed following its historic
flight to the moon;
December, 1972.

The Cernan Corp.

Small pieces of the outer skin from Command Module America, *encased in Lucite and presented to the author by Gene Cernan.*

Photo of Apollo 17 astronaut Schmitt taken by his fellow crewman Gene Cernan while on the lunar surface.

Golf Team in recognition of his lunar golf shots, and the guests there included former heavy weight boxing champion Joe Louis.

That night Shepard addressed the annual banquet meeting of the American Newspaper Publishers Association (ANPA). It was during this trip we began talking about his return to East Derry, New Hampshire, where he was born and raised and where he had been honored after the historic flight in 1961. East Derry can be cold and the weather unpredictable in April, but planning officials were insistent on a parade and a series of appearances.

Proposed events were discussed and approved by Al. He and wife Louise arrived on Thursday, April 1, aboard a commercial flight that arrived at Boston's Logan Field. They were welcomed by a delegation from East Derry and the state of New Hampshire. A motorcade to the home of his parents followed, where they enjoyed a family dinner and prepared for a busy Friday schedule.

The day began with remarks before members of the New Hampshire Senate and House at the state house in Concord, and at an assembly of students from Derry's Pinkerton Academy, his alma mater.

Saturday dawned bitter and cold, but Shepard and Louise rode at the head of the parade and were then seated, where for two hours they reviewed the nearly 80 marching bands and floats from all over New England.

Despite the frequent snowflakes and bone chilling winds, Al and Louise remained seated for the entire parade. During the course of our stay, he had been frequently mentioned as a candidate for the U.S. Senate from New Hampshire, but made it known then and thereafter, he had no interest in politics.

He remained with NASA and returned as chief of the astronaut office in June 1971, a position he had relinquished to Apollo 10 astronaut Tom Stafford in 1969, when he was selected to command Apollo 14.

He and the crew made one final appearance as guests of The White House News Photographers black tie annual dinner in Washington on April 28, 1971.

A few days later, he and Louise participated in dedication ceremonies commemorating the tenth anniversary of his historic sub orbital 15 minute Mercury Redstone 3 flight on May 5, 1961 from the Cape Kennedy Air Force Station.

In 1974 he retired from the U.S. Navy as a vice admiral and from NASA and eventually moved to Pebble Beach, California, where he operated his Seven Fourteen company, named after his two space flights, and played a lot of golf. Meanwhile, he and Slayton had coauthored a book, "Moon Shot".

Slayton died in 1993 of a brain tumor before publication of the book. I was delighted to accept when Al asked me and Jack King to introduce him at a book signing in Arlington, Virginia, on July 20, 1994, about two months after I had retired from NASA. Ironically, it was 25 years to the day of the first lunar landing in 1969. As a thank you, he presented me with an autographed copy of the book with an inscription, "To Gene—Thanks for being a part of this!" Al Shepard.

It was almost four years to the day later on July 21, 1998 when he died at age 74 from complications of Leukemia, which had been diagnosed two years earlier. His wife of 53 years, Louise, died of a heart attack a month later while flying from San Francisco to her Monterey home. The couple had been married for 53 years and had three daughters.

Four years earlier in 1994, Roosa became the first member of that crew to die of complications from pancreatitis. He had retired from the Air Force and NASA in 1976 and with the help of Shepard, was able to acquire a Coors beer distributorship in Gulfport, Mississippi.

Mitchell, who became the sixth man to walk on the Moon, was the last member of the crew to die in a Florida hospice facility on Thursday, February 4, 2016, the day before the anniversary of his lunar landing. A U.S. Navy Captain, aeronautical engineer, and test pilot, he had earned two bachelor degrees and was an MIT graduate.

I was fortunate to have worked with both Roosa in Georgia and Mitchell in South Carolina, during their "Weeks in the Barrel". While with NASA, Mitchell had acquired an interest in ESP and spoke openly of his belief in UFO's. Following his retirement from the Navy as a Captain and from the astronaut corps in 1972, he founded the Institute of Noetic Sciences.

With the conclusion of the Apollo 14 activities, we began preparations for the three remaining Apollo launches. Veteran Astronaut Dave Scott commanded an all Air Force Apollo 15 crew with rookies Jim Irwin, the lunar module pilot and Al Worden, command module pilot.

Both Worden and Irwin had been "Week in the Barrel" participants in 1968, so were somewhat aware of public and media demands.

Apollo 15 launched on July 26, 1971 and was the first mission on which the lunar rover was used. It enabled Scott and Irwin to traverse the surface and explore the geology of the Hadley Rille/Appennine region of the Moon and travel much further than the three previous landings.

The mission ended successfully on August 7 with the splashdown of *Endeavour*, despite the failure of one of the three parachutes to fully deploy, and the landing was a little harder than the previous missions. The astronauts were not aware of the incident until they were almost ready to hit the ocean.

It soon became apparent the scientific results of the mission exceeded those of the previous three landings and was generating broad interest from the science community here and abroad. The Department of State and the U.S. Information Agency were proposing a two week scientific "Mission to Europe" by the crew to Stockholm, Rome/Milan, Paris, London/Cambridge and Munich, where the crew would share their findings with the help of a video presentation.

The European trip would be after the culmination of a series of U.S. appearances that summer and fall, including a week of events in Utah where the astronauts spoke on behalf of two prominent Utahans, NASA Administrator James Fletcher, and Senator Frank Moss, the powerful Democratic chairman of the U.S. Senate Committee of Aeronautics and Space.

This was followed by a trip to New York for a ticker tape parade, receipt of keys to the city by Mayor John Lindsay and numerous appearances with former President George H.W. Bush, who was still serving as the U.S. Ambassador to the United Nations. He and Secretary General U. co-hosted a reception.

It was about this time that NASA was in discussions with Special Air Missions at Andrews Air Force Base for the use of a charter aircraft. It was one of the few times a jet was not available, but a seldom-used C-118, military version of the civilian DC-6, was offered for the trip.

We later learned of the plane's historical significance. While semi-retired, the C-118 had served as the first "Air Force One" by former Presidents Truman and Eisenhower before being replaced by a Boeing 707 jet just before the election of President Kennedy in 1960.

Scott was unhappy over the decision, but the slower flying aircraft performed well and was not an issue until a member of the press at one of our stops inquired why three men who had flown and landed on the Moon were traveling in a piston-powered airliner.

I was selected as the public affairs officer for the trip. In discussing presentation items, Scott suggested a plaque with a flown mission patch and core samples removed by engineers from *Endeavour*'s heat shield and embedded in Lucite shaped in the cone form of the *Endeavour* command module.

We began the trip with six of the items for presentation to the United Nations, Pope Paul VI and other foreign dignitaries. The Pope was very interested in the astronaut's mission and graciously accepted one of the plaques. While not included in the audience, the Pope took time to welcome everyone in the group and presented each with a Rosary.

It was during the trip that news reports began to circulate that the crew had taken 398 unauthorized commemorative postage stamp covers with them. One hundred were to be sold to the German stamp dealer who had provided them. Although taking souvenirs into space was not illegal, pre-approval by NASA was required.

Discovery of the covers led to a congressional investigation and disciplinary action against the three. Scott became deputy director of the NASA Flight Research Center at Edwards AFB, later becoming the director. Worden was transferred to the NASA Ames Research Center, and Irwin resigned from the U.S. Air Force and NASA to form a" High Flight" religious ministry in Colorado.

Worden later filed suit against NASA for return of the covers, citing the partnership between NASA and the U.S. Postal Service to sell covers flown aboard the Space Shuttle. The courts agreed and the covers were returned.

My relations with all three remained good and unchanged during and after I retired. Scott was director of the Dryden Flight Research Center at Edwards during the test flights of the *Enterprise* and later the landings of the *Columbia* and *Challenger* Space Shuttles. I also played a few rounds of golf with Worden after his retirement and move to Vero Beach, Florida, and with Irwin during the time he headed "High Flight" and until his untimely death in 1991. Scott was especially thoughtful, on my retirement, giving me an inscribed Apollo 15 patch on a piece of the beta cloth used in the astronaut flights suits.

Plans for the launch of Apollo 16 were taking place in late 1971 and early 1972. It was scheduled to be the next to last mission in the Apollo program. Veteran Gemini and Apollo astronaut John W. Young would be the commander. He would be joined by two rookie astronauts: T.K. Mattingly, who had been scheduled as the command pilot for Apollo 13 before being replaced by Jack Swigert, and Charlie Duke as the lunar module pilot.

It marked my second experience working with Young. He had been the command module pilot on Apollo 10, and joined fellow astronauts Tom Stafford and Gene Cernan and their wives for the trip to New York.

Between then and the months prior to Apollo 16, Young and his wife Barbara had divorced. Long hours of training resulting in weeks away from his family were generally blamed for the breakup after a 16-year marriage and two children.

His second marriage was to Susy Feldman, secretary to a space contractor in St. Louis. Young was quoted as saying years later after he commanded the first Space Shuttle flight," she's the best thing that ever happened to me." When asked what he considered to be his greatest achievement, he responded: "I have no idea, but my smartest achievement was when Suzy and I got married."

They remained happily married until Young died unexpectedly January 5, 2018, at his home in Houston at age 87. The cause of death was complications from pneumonia. He was the longest serving astronaut, becoming the first person to fly six space missions during Gemini, Apollo and Space Shuttle programs and was considered to be the best engineer and test pilot of all the astronauts in a career that spanned 42 years.

In 2005, NASA named him Ambassador of Exploration, recognizing his contributions that included 13 years as chief of the astronaut office and other administrative positions providing advice, and counsel on technical, operational and safety matters.

Apollo 16 was launched on April 16, 1972, and Young and Duke became the second crew to use the lunar rover. The mission lasted a little more than eleven days including the seventy-one hours on the lunar surface, during which they logged twenty hours and fourteen minutes in the LM, and gathered geologically older lunar material than the samples obtained in the first four landings.

With splashdown of Apollo 16, on April 27, 1972, my associate Stretch Flanagan and I began preparing what would become the most ambitious schedule of public appearances by any astronaut crew. The first of crew and individual appearances began in May and continued well beyond the agreed three-month period of post flight scheduling.

It was decided to schedule appearances Tuesday through Thursday, enabling the astronauts to spend the weekends back in Houston. The use of a twelve-passenger NASA Gulfstream turbo prop made our scheduling and planning much easier. While slower than commercial jets, the planes provided more flexibility and convenience for the crew, wives and support team.

Mattingly, remembered for the role he played during Apollo 13, joined John and Suzy and Charlie and Dotti during most of the appearances, but was concerned for the welfare of his wife Elizabeth, who was in Houston awaiting the birth of their first child.

Requests were discussed by phone with Young and written schedules were faxed to the astronaut office well in advance of the appearances. Cities were selected, and schedules were developed. The post flight usually began with a trip to Washington, where the crew would call on the President and make a presentation.

This was followed by a series of appearances before key congressional committees, including a reception hosted by Congressman Olin (Tiger) Teague, the powerful chairman of the House Committee on aeronautics and space, who became after Audie Murphy, the most decorated U.S. combat soldier of World War II, with three purple hearts, three silver stars and three bronze stars. He was a champion of veteran issues, but was even better known for his strong support of the space program.

He had personally hired Swigert following the Apollo 13 mission and tour as the executive director of his committee, a position he held until his resignation and move to Colorado, where he ran an unsuccessful race as a Republican for a U.S. Senate seat.

Years later he was elected a Republican member of the U.S. House of Representatives, but died at Georgetown Hospital in Washington of cancer on December 27, 1982, less than a month before being sworn in. I felt badly when I learned of his death, especially because while I had planned a visit, I never did and was left feeling guilty.

I immediately made plans to attend his funeral in Denver, and called on Lovell for details. He and Marilyn had just returned to Chicago from a skiing vacation in Europe, and said he would be flying his company's private plane and invited me to join them on the flight to Denver.

He offered to meet my flight and was easy to spot because his arm was in a sling from a skiing accident. We drove to his home in Lake Forest where I spent the night, and we departed the next morning for Denver.

Many of Jack's astronaut colleagues were there for the Catholic Church services and burial and the reception that followed. Congressman Don Fuqua, who had replaced Olin Teague as chairman of the House space and technology committee, had flown a charter aircraft and was there with committee members.

As the schedule of appearances for Apollo 16 began to develop, Flanagan and I alternated advance and staffing assignments. For example, I would travel to a stop, meet the arriving aircraft, introduce the astronauts to the welcoming committee, and remain until the conclusion of the events then depart to the next stop, where Flanagan would be waiting having already completed arrangements for the visit.

I remember one such occasion where Stretch had advanced an appearance by the crew in Louisville, Kentucky. He was there with the mayor and other officials including Colonel Harland Sanders, the fried chicken legend, when our aircraft touched down. Following the greetings and introductions, the astronaut party got into waiting convertible limousines for a luncheon in downtown Louisville.

Our motorcade passed by the University and I heard a student yell, "there's Colonel Sanders, he gets into everything." Young was not amused when he realized Sanders had unwittingly used his celebrity status to join the astronaut party. It was even funnier when Young, straight faced, said, "Stretch, we didn't come to Kentucky to sell fried chicken."

Another incident worth mentioning was the crew's visit to San Francisco and an appearance before the prestigious World Affairs Council, whose members included Shirley Temple Black. It was in the limousine on our way to the event that Mattingly, who often questioned a particular appearance and our public affairs rationale, asked Stretch what he was expected to say.

Stretch, trying to be helpful, responded that the group was interested in world affairs and would like to know more about the space program. Mattingly grinned and replied, I could say the same thing about sex. Stretch countered with, "I suggest you stick to something you know about." As we all broke into laughter, Mattingly responded, "That's the second best put down ever, the best will be when I get you."

While Mayor John Lindsay had invited the Apollo 16 astronauts to New York, George H.W. Bush, who was still the U.S. Ambassador to the United Nations, extended an invitation for the crew to visit the U.N. and make presentations. The visit would include a reception hosted by Bush and Secretary General U Thant.

Thanks to Mr. Bush, we were able to stay at the Waldorf Astoria, where he and Mrs. Bush resided. Also living there was Mrs. Jean MacArthur, widow of the famous General of the Army, Douglas MacArthur.

Mrs. MacArthur conveyed to Bush that she wanted to host a dinner for the astronauts in her penthouse. Following the dinner, the group would attend a showing of the Broadway show, "Something Funny Happened to Me on the Way to the Forum", starring comedian Phil Silvers, who received a best actor Tony for his performance.

When it came time to escort the astronauts, I reluctantly rang the doorbell to her suite. She, accompanied by Ambassador Bush, greeted me graciously and invited me in to a room filled with hundreds of items she and the General had possessed since their storybook marriage in 1937.

As I stood there, I couldn't describe my feelings. I had grown up during the war years and recall the role of General MacArthur and how he, Mrs. MacArthur and their young son Arthur were ordered by President Roosevelt in 1942 to leave the Philippines on a PT boat for Australia when it became apparent that Corregidor was about to fall to the Japanese.

I knew the General had been a controversial figure, beginning with his role in the breakup of the "Bonus Marchers" in Washington, D.C. in 1932. While he kept his "I Shall Return" pledge to return to the Philippines in 1944, some charged it was a grandstand play as he was photographed wading ashore.

But after accepting the Japanese surrender in September, 1945, he oversaw the occupation and rebuilding of the country, and was credited with sweeping economic, political and social changes. He was named commander of U.N. Forces in 1950 during the Korean War until he was relieved of command by President Truman.

History will remember Mrs. MacArthur as a devoted wife and defender of her husband's controversial legacy. She was presented the

Presidential Medal of Freedom by President Reagan in 1988. In making the presentation, he called her a" shining example, a woman of substance and character, a loyal wife and mother and like her general, a patriot."

To this day, I cherish the experience of being in a room filled with so much history, and was quickly able to understand why Mrs. MacArthur was held in such high regard for her personal and financial support of the arts, theater and philanthropic activities in New York. She died in 2000 at the age of 101.

My 27-year career with NASA was marked by so many memorable events and places involving so many distinguished individuals, but the opportunity to be greeted personally by Mrs. MacArthur and spend even a few minutes in a room filled with so much history ranks right near the top.

In the days and weeks that followed our New York stay, we managed to complete a hectic and demanding schedule. After New York, the crew accepted an invitation to visit Hartford and Bridgeport, Connecticut, where many NASA Apollo contractors were located.

The highlight of the visit was the crew's meeting with Igor Sikorsky, the Russian/American aviation legend who pioneered the development of the helicopter and fixed wing aircraft. Ironically, Sikorsky died a few months after the visit in October at the age of 83. The chance for the crew, especially Young, who began his Navy career flying helicopters, was a seminal moment for the lunar astronauts and Sikorsky.

Young performed like a real trooper during our many travels. I believe he was greatly influenced by Suzy, who often expressed concern that we were working her Johnny too hard. Charlie and Dotti Duke were just happy to enjoy the experience and the opportunity to travel the country and receive so many accolades from an admiring public.

I felt that Mattingly greatly underestimated his talents as a public speaker. He almost always spoke extemporaneously, and knew his subject well.

He was commander of STS-4, the fourth and final test flight of the orbiter *Columbia*. His final mission was STS-51-C, the first use of the shuttle for the Department of Defense. He left NASA and earned a rear admiral promotion before retiring from the U.S. Navy in 1985.

I remember one experience worth recalling during our New York stay. Stretch and I were busy in our Waldorf suite one afternoon preparing presentation items that required inscriptions and autographs for events that night. Time was of the essence, and we knocked on the door of the Young suite.

When Suzy answered, I asked if we could get John to inscribe and sign some photographs. It was mid-afternoon and she replied, "Johnny and I are taking a nap". When I suggested that we just needed a few minutes and for her to resume her nap, she sharply responded, "We don't take naps alone." Upon hearing the exchange, John appeared in his bathrobe, grabbed a pen, and signed the items. I can only presume that he and Suzy resumed their nap, together.

There were other appearances, including events in Orlando, Florida, John's hometown. Included in the homecoming was the dedication of a section of highway, named "The John Young Parkway."

I am most proud of an autographed photo I received from the Apollo 16 crew following the completion of the post flight schedule. The item, which includes an American flag and a patch, both flown on the mission, includes John's personal inscription which reads: "To Gene with many thanks for your support of the Apollo 16 post flight appearances to 33 to 36 places in 18-to 20s states and DC. Warmest personal regards from the crew of Apollo 16."

My relationship with John would continue, first when he replaced Alan Shepard as chief of the astronaut office two years later in 1974, and when he was named as the commander of STS-1, the first launch of the Space Shuttle *Columbia* in 1981 and the post flight that followed that mission.

Chapter Fifteen

WRAPPING UP THE APOLLO PROGRAM

As Apollo 16 activities came to a conclusion, we were already making preparations for the final Apollo launch 17 scheduled for early December of 1972, to be the first night launch in the history of the program. Veteran Gemini and Apollo astronaut Gene Cernan would be the commander, and Ron Evans would serve as the command module pilot.

For awhile, it appeared that Joe Engle would be the lunar module pilot, but after considerable pressure from the scientific community who had been lobbying for a geologist to have a chance to study the lunar surface, Dr. Harrison (Jack) Schmitt, who was among the first scientist astronauts selected by NASA in 1965, replaced Engle and would land with Cernan and become the next to last person to depart the lunar surface.

It became apparent that the final Apollo liftoff would match, or even exceed, the media and public interest in Apollo 11. A record number of requests for press accreditations were issued, and thousands of launch invitations were issued by our office and NASA field offices.

An estimated 300 charter buses would be needed to transport a record number of special guests to the viewing site located near the Vehicle Assembly Building and about three and a half miles from the 36-A launch site.

In addition, an estimated 7,000 vehicle passes were issued to the general public, which would again enable entire families to drive on to the Kennedy Center Parkway and Causeway and view the liftoff from about seven miles away. Like the previous launches, thousands of people found viewing locations in nearby locations along the Banana and Indian Rivers and Atlantic Ocean beaches. Many watched from as far as Orlando as the liftoff lit up the sky for miles.

While missing the thrill of the actual liftoff and the sounds it created, those viewing the launch from these sites had a much better view of staging as the Saturn V roared down range and achieved orbit.

More than 12,000, including world leaders, members of the United Nations, members of Congress, representatives of federal agencies and state and local officials and other dignitaries were there for the historic launch. Vice President Spiro Agnew, who had attended most of the previous Apollo liftoffs, represented President Nixon and his group included Frank Sinatra.

The launch countdown proceeded normally until technical difficulties caused a two-hour and 40 minute delay. Finally, the crew was informed it was go for launch and liftoff occurred at 12:33 a.m. on December 7, ironically, the 31st anniversary of the attack on Pearl Harbor.

The liftoff was the first to occur after dark and the ignition illuminated the sky as the Saturn roared to life and began its journey down range with the final landing four days later.

Cernan and Schmitt used the lunar rover to explore the Taurus-Littrow landing site, which had been selected because it was thought the astronauts would find rocks and soil samples older than those returned by earlier crews. Cernan and Schmitt were the eleventh and twelfth men to land on the Moon, while command module pilot Ron Evans remained in orbit waiting for their return.

Cernan will be remembered for his eloquent remarks as he prepared to climb up the lunar ladder for the last time. "As I take man's last step from the surface, back home for some time to come—but we believe not too long into the future—I'd like to just say what I believe history will record. That America's challenge of today has forged man's destiny of tomorrow. And, as we leave the Moon at Taurus-Littrow, we leave as we came and, God willing, as we shall return, with peace and hope for all mankind. God Speed, the crew of Apollo 17."

He will be always be remembered as the last man on the Moon, but also for his gesture before climbing the ladder back into the LM, dropping to one knee and etching his daughter's initials "TDC" Tracy Dawn Cernan on the moon's surface.

With splashdown on December 19, we were already at work on a domestic post flight schedule that would begin after the holidays in January and continue until April. Gene and wife Barbara Cernan, Ron and wife Jan Evans and bachelor Jack Schmitt, would begin the tour with a trip to Los Angles for Super Bowl VII on January 14, 1973.

I had gotten to know Gene and Barbara briefly after Apollo 10, but it was a new experience getting to know Ron and Jan Evans. Jack was a bachelor, so there would be no spousal issues with him. Barbara and Jan wanted Stretch and I to know that they were there to support their husbands and would do everything possible to make our jobs easy.

Word had reached them that some of the wives had complained about the role public affairs expected them to play. Stretch and I were not disappointed, because we found Barbara and Jan the very best to work with during our many travels.

Dick Gordon, who had flown on Apollo 12, was now an executive with the NFL's New Orleans Saints, and was instrumental in arranging for the crew to receive an invitation from Commissioner Pete Rozelle to participate in Super Bowl VII activities before the game between the Washington Redskins and the undefeated Miami Dolphins in the Los Angeles Coliseum.

On game day they were introduced as they rode around the infield in an open convertible, wearing red, white and blue turtleneck sweaters, and then led the crowd in the reciting of the national anthem.

It was a game that will be remembered as the one where the Dolphins won 14-7 to become the only NFL team to complete a season undefeated and win the Super Bowl.

The crew remained in Los Angeles, and the next day traveled to Pasadena where they thanked employees at the NASA Jet Propulsion Laboratory, whose work was known worldwide, much of it contributing to the success of the Apollo program.

The following day, the NASA Gulfstream flew the astronauts back to Houston, where they were able to spend a few days before departing once again, this time to Washington, to participate in the second Inauguration of President Nixon.

It was a cold blustery day as the crew rode in an open convertible down Pennsylvania Avenue and past the White House reviewing stand where they waved back at a smiling Nixon. Little did they know then that an investigation would soon begin leading to Watergate and Nixon's resignation in 1974.

The Super Bowl was the first of what would be a world-wind tour by the crew to fifty-three cities in twenty-nine states between January and March, 1973. Stretch and I staffed many of the appearances much the same way we had Apollo 16; advance, staff and hopscotch city to city.

A typical week began on Tuesday when the astronauts would depart Houston in a Gulfstream and arrive in Little Rock, Arkansas. I had arrived a day earlier to complete arrangements with our hosts. The welcoming group included Governor Dale Bumpers, the mayor and others. A motorcade followed, and then a civic luncheon followed by visits to schools, and that we night attended a private dinner hosted by Governor Bumpers in his mansion.

After an overnight stay, the astronauts departed for Chattanooga, Tennessee, where Stretch was there with the welcoming committee. It was almost a repeat of the Little Rock schedule. Meanwhile, I had departed that morning for Atlanta to complete arrangements for the crew to address a meeting of the Georgia legislature and a personal meeting with then Governor Jimmy Carter, who was already being mentioned as a candidate for president in 1976.

Chicago Mayor Richard Daley invited the crew to Chicago, where they would be honored as special guests for the 73rd annual St. Patrick's Day parade and banquet on Saturday, March 17. The trip coincided with Cernan's 39th birthday on the 14th. It was an opportunity to combine the two events in Chicago and his hometown in nearby Bellwood.

The demanding schedule of appearances was beginning to take its toll. While most of the travel was accomplished using the NASA Gulfstream's, days were long and grueling, especially when it was necessary to fly aboard commercial flights. A final week of appearances was arranged in late March for Montana, Washington and Idaho. We first stopped in Billings, where the astronauts spoke before a civic luncheon and an assembly at Eastern Montana College.

We then left for my hometown, Great Falls, where I had arranged a schedule with two former bosses, Al Donohue, of KMON Radio and Dan Snyder of KRTV, both well known and respected. They agreed to organize a dinner at the Meadowlark Country Club, with an audience of civic and business leaders.

The country club dinner was a stag affair and a free evening for the wives. Our hosts had arranged for an informal dinner for them at the renovated Milwaukee Road Train Station, a famous landmark in Great Falls that Snyder had converted into a restaurant and gift boutique.

Barbara and Jan had tired of the rubber chicken circuit, and for me it was an opportunity for them to have a home-cooked meal. Who better to prepare and serve the meal than my own mother at the home of my parents, Minnie and Gino Marianetti in nearby Black Eagle?

My mother prepared a delicious home cooked meal of spaghetti, Cornish game hens stuffed with wild rice, garlic bread and a frozen dessert. The wives sent their hostess bouquets of yellow and white mums along with a signed photo of the Apollo 17 launch, which my parents had watched in person.

The following morning the astronauts conducted a news conference and then appeared live on the city's two TV stations, KFBB and KRTV. At noon, we departed for Seattle, where they were honored at a civic luncheon at the Pacific Science Center, and then thanked workers at the Boeing facility for their efforts in developing and building the first stage of the Saturn V rocket.

A trip to Boise occurred on Friday, March 30, where the astronauts addressed the Idaho Legislature and then enjoyed a luncheon with Governor Cecil Andrus. The final appearance was scheduled the following Monday in Helena, Montana.

With a free weekend, the astronaut party spent the weekend as guests of a Sun Valley, Idaho resort owner, who kindly offered use of the facility. It was a rare chance to relax and ski.

On Monday, we left Sun Valley, departed for Helena and were met on arrival by Governor Tom Judge and other state and local officials and then hosted at a Capitol luncheon. Judge and Cernan developed a personal friendship, and after leaving NASA made frequent trips back to Montana and campaigned for Judge when he ran for re-election.

The Helena visit marked the official end of the Apollo 17 post flight. The last two Apollo crews had visited nearly every state, where they were able to share their unique experiences with the people who had paid for and supported the Apollo program.

It was now early April, and I was honored to receive the first of what would be three NASA Exceptional Service Awards presented by three NASA Administrators. I received a second in 1981 and the third in 1990.

Rumors were circulating that President Nixon was preparing to send the Apollo 17 astronauts to Africa and Asia, and Cernan had requested that I be part of a three-person advance team that would include a NASA security representative and someone from the U.S. Information Agency (USIA.)

Charlie Buckley, who had been the director of security at the Kennedy Space Center for many years, was selected to travel with me to coordinate security. We departed Washington around mid-May and visited U.S. embassy and consulates in Nairobi, Kenya; Dakar, Senegal; Niamey, Niger; Lagos, Nigeria; Yaounde, Cameroon; and Abidjan, capital of the Ivory Coast.

Working with embassy officials, schedules were developed for each stop and cabled to the U.S. State Department in Washington, where they were reviewed and forwarded to the astronauts. Our advance work was completed in two weeks, and we were prepared to meet the Apollo 17 party in Los Palmas, Canary Islands, on June 1, where we would start the month-long tour a day later.

Charlie and I had begun our advance trip on a Pan Am flight from New York to London's Heathrow Airport, where we transferred to a BOAC flight to Kenya, Nairobi. The flight required a refueling stop at Entebbe in Uganda. It's hard to believe, but we were the only two passengers on the flight. Just before landing, the lone flight attendant advised us to remain on board, given the reputation of the country's president Idi Amin, who had seized power in a military coup in 1971.

He was especially suspicious of foreigners, and anyone carrying a camera was quickly arrested. Charlie and I decided to stretch our legs and left the airplane for the visitors lounge. The terminal was crowded with curious onlookers, but we had no problem re-boarding and continuing to our first stop in Nairobi.

We had no way of knowing then that three years later this would be the site of an Israeli commando raid to free more than 246 mainly Jewish and Israeli hostages from a hijacked Air France flight aircraft who were being held by Palestinian hijackers. The event was later made into a made for TV movie, "Operation Entebbe" in 1976 starring actor Peter Finch, and into a theater movie, "7 Days in Entebbe" in March 2018.

I had one really freighting moment during our advance trips I believe worth mentioning. Our final flight on the advance trip from Dakar, Senegal, to the Canary Islands was aboard a French-made Caravelle, an early mid-size jet with a crash history. I recall the pilot using the entire length of the runway to achieve liftoff. Seated in a window seat, I watched anxiously as the wheels retracted and the Pacific Ocean came into view below me. Wow!

The U.S. C-135 Air Force plane carrying the astronaut's party touched down on schedule and Charlie and I were there for the welcome and the drive to our guest quarters at the U.S. military base at

Gando, Las Palmas. The party included the astronauts, and wives, along with staffers and security.

Dee O'Hara, a registered nurse whose NASA origins dated back to the early days of the space program where she earned a reputation for her work in the medical and physical testing of the original Mercury astronauts and those that followed, had been added to our group.

I recall one experience related by the late Mercury Astronaut Wally Schirra, in Tom Wolfe's book, "The Right Stuff." When asked for a urine sample during a routine physical, Schirra, who had a reputation as a practical joker, handed her a vial of beer.

My memories of the trip are filled with similar experiences, like flying aboard a Cameroon Air Force C-7A Caribou over some of the most desolate jungle terrain I have ever seen. I remember many of our flights during the advance trips were flown aboard foreign carriers using U.S. made Boeing 727, aircraft where passengers were allowed to fly with goats and flammable products. Each time it was a life and death experience, and I thank the Lord I survived.

Another event worth sharing occurred during our brief stay in Abidjan, the French-speaking Capitol of the Ivory Coast, which had gained its independence from France in 1960. Our group was staying at the Hotel Ivoire, one of the truly premiere hotels in West Africa. Built as a show place, it housed eleven tennis courts, swimming pools, casinos, restaurants, grocery store, nightclubs, sauna and even a bowling alley. It was the one place where you could get a real American hamburger, which wasn't cheap.

We had made reservations for our group to enjoy dinner at one of the city's exclusive restaurants. As often happened, a heavy rainstorm occurred just as our motorcade was leaving the hotel. The rain continued nonstop, and flooding soon became a problem. On arrival we received a warm welcome and were escorted to our reserved dining room.

While enjoying a round of drinks and getting ready to place our dinner orders, it was Barbara Cernan who pointed at the ceiling and screeched, "Oh, my God, it's a rat!" My first reaction was it must be a bat. But as I looked skyward, sure enough it was a large real life rat, which had scurried to higher ground to evade the flooding of the outside storm. I recall the owner-bartender and his look of amazement as if to say, this happens all the time.

The story has a happy ending. Not everyone was able to enjoy their meal, but Gene Cernan laughingly said, "Be thankful we saw the rat before we ate." Needless to say, most everyone selected non-meat items from the menu.

Between June and early July, we had traveled across Africa and South East Asia with stops in Senegal, Niger, Nigeria, Ivory Coast, Cameroon, Kenya, Pakistan, India, Singapore, Indonesia, Bali, the Philippines, and Saipan in the Northern Mariana Islands and Majuro in the Marshall Islands.

I am left with some wonderful memories of the trip including the opportunity to visit one of the wonders of the world, the Taj Mahal, in Agra, India. The crew made appearances on the islands of Saipan and Tinian, while our Air Force charter flew to Guam for supplies and fuel.

Our hosts provided briefings and explained the brutal fighting between the occupying Japanese forces, as well as how important the airfields were for the B-29 Superfortress aircraft to conduct bombing raids on Japan beginning in 1944.

I clearly remember seeing from my motel room the remains of a U.S. tank with its gun turret still visible about 100 yards from shore, a clear reminder of the invasion that had occurred twenty-nine years earlier.

The long flight back to Houston included a brief refueling stop in Honolulu, where for me it was an opportunity to visit Pearl Harbor and see the USS Arizona Memorial. I had just turned six years old and my father had taken me to a movie on December 7, 1941. We first learned of the Japanese attack when we returned home, and it is a memory I have never forgotten.

It is difficult to describe my feelings as we arrived at the memorial and listened to a tour guide explain the circumstances and the significance of the event. Pearl Harbor, the Kennedy Assassination and 9/11, are moments in a lifetime that one never forgets.

With the conclusion of the trip, I was able to slowly adjust to the time changes and after a brief vacation, was able to resume my work at NASA Headquarters. Just before leaving on the advance trip, I had worked the launch of Skylab at the Kennedy Space Center, and NASA program officials were in the process of working on a solution to salvage the Skylab vehicle that had been damaged during liftoff.

The launch of Pete Conrad and his crew on Skylab 2 to repair the damaged spacecraft occurred while I was in India, and we were able to listen to a U.S. Embassy radio describing the liftoff. For me, it was the first time I had missed seeing a live Apollo launch liftoff during my NASA career.

Thankfully, Conrad and his crew of Paul Weitz and Joe Kerwin were able to stabilize Skylab and repair the solar panels that were damaged at liftoff and install a parasol to protect the exposed station from the intense solar heat. Conrad was later honored for his role when he received one of the first Space Medal of Honor medals.

Like the previous crews, we began to schedule Skylab 2 appearances, beginning in New York City and a presentation to New York Governor Nelson Rockefeller. Other stops included Augusta, Maine; Baton Rouge, Louisiana; and Montgomery, Alabama, where the astronauts attended a dinner hosted by Governor George Wallace and his wife Cornelia in the Governor's mansion.

As we concluded our series of public appearances, I was sorry to learn that Pete Conrad would be retiring soon from the Navy and NASA to accept a senior management position with then McDonnell Douglas Aircraft.

I remember once handing Conrad a schedule for the day's events and his smiling reply. "What's this?" he asked and I replied, "Today's schedule."

"Hell, I don't need this," he said. "Just point me where you want me and tell me how long to speak."

While retired, we managed to see each other many times over the years and he was always the same with those unruly eyebrows that he never seemed to trim. Pete and his wife Jane later divorced and both remarried. He died of injuries incurred in a motorcycle accident in 1999, and I attended his services at the Fort Myer Chapel at Arlington National Cemetery.

Country singer and a personal friend Willie Nelson appeared without an introduction during the service and sang "Amazing Grace", then exited through a side door without saying a word. Pete loved country music and he carried into space cassette tapes of songs recorded by Nelson, Charlie Pride and other country and bluegrass singers. In fact, he and Pride were close friends and Charlie and his wife were Pete's personal guests at his Apollo 12 launch. Many of his astronaut colleagues attended, including Armstrong, who introduced me to his second wife, Carol.

Two Skylab missions remained. Alan Bean, who had walked on the moon with Conrad on Apollo 12, commanded the second mission with two rookies, Jack Lousma and Owen Garriott. The three spent more than fifty-nine days in space. *Note: Owen passed away on April 15, 2019.*

Skylab 4 was the third and final mission in the program. It featured an all rookie crew, all making their first space flights. U.S. Marine Colonel Gerry Carr was the commander, U.S. Air Force Colonel Bill Pogue and a civilian, Dr. Ed Gibson were his crewmates. Before a successful splashdown, the astronauts had spent a record of more than eighty-four days in space.

Like the astronauts before them, the nine made crew and individual appearances to cities, universities and NASA contractor plants all over the U.S.

While I accompanied the astronauts on a number of the appearances, one with Alan Bean comes to mind.

I had arranged for him to fly to Boston, where we would meet and make day trips to nearby New England capital cities. We stayed at the Parker House in downtown Boston, famous for its "Parker House Rolls". Our first stop was at Springfield, the Massachusetts capital, followed by stops in Hartford, Connecticut; Montpelier, Vermont; and Providence, Rhode Island.

Al made presentations to the state governors and some of the legislatures, and spoke at several civic luncheons and banquets. His talks featured his experiences on Apollo 12 and Skylab 3. I always felt that Al, along with several of his fellow astronauts, was a most gifted speaker and later a renowned artist.

I recall an evening at our Boston hotel where we were booked in adjacent rooms. As we said goodnight, Al noticed that I left my oxford shoes where they would be picked up and shined by the hotel concierge, then left for me the following morning.

When I said I would be paying $2 for the service, he smiled and said next time, leave them at my door along with the $2. We have had many a laugh over that exchange, and he will be the first to admit that he is not cheap, just frugal.

Later that year, I again began working with Bean, who had been assigned the responsibility of escorting a group of Soviet Cosmonauts visiting the U.S. to learn and understand the workings of the U.S. space program in preparation for the joint Apollo/Soyuz mission in July 1975. Stretch and I began developing places to visit including Mount Vernon, Arlington National Cemetery and other tourist points of interest.

The visit to Arlington included laying a wreath at the gravesites of Gus Grissom and Roger Chaffee. One evening we sailed the Potomac River aboard the presidential yacht *Sequoia*, which the White House gave us permission to use.

Once comfortable with the schedule of events, Bean would excuse himself and visit the National Art Gallery and other DC museums and galleries. He then confirmed his desire to become an artist and wanted to see and learn from the many of the classic works of art on display. His dream of becoming an artist is described in his 1998 book, "Apollo: An Eyewitness Account by Astronaut/Explorer Artist/Moonwalker Alan Bean."

I hadn't realized that during his early years as Navy test pilot, he enrolled in art classes and his dream of eventually became a reality when he resigned from NASA at the age of 49 and dedicated himself as an accomplished artist. Fellow astronaut Gene Cernan once described him as "The Michelangelo of the Space Age." Many of his works are considered priceless and are on display in museums and galleries everywhere.

Included in the book's dedication is his tribute to Pete Conrad. It reads partially, "to Pete Conrad, my primary role model, who saw the possibilities within me and who allowed me to achieve the dream I had of being a good astronaut."

Bean, who was the fourth man to walk on the Moon, died unexpectedly on May 26, 2018 in a Houston hospital shortly after a trip to Fort Wayne, Indiana. Family and friends gathered at Arlington National Cemetery on November 8, where he was laid to rest with full military honors and a Missing Man Flyover, and reunited with Conrad and Gordon who were buried there earlier.

I had developed a personal relationship with Bean after Apollo 12, and he spent two nights as a guest in our Alexandria home in 1974.

He had flown to Andrews Air Force Base in a T-38 following a trip to Delaware, where he was working on redesign of a space suit and was able to combine that trip with a stop in Washington to attend the presentation and receipt of the prestigious Harmon Trophy being presented to all three Skylab crews.

I agreed to meet his flight, and extended an invitation to stay at our home as a guest. He accepted and was treated to a home cooked Italian dinner prepared by Mrs. Marianetti. His love of Italian food was well known in the astronaut community, especially spaghetti and meat balls, which he enjoyed in our Alexandria home. Mrs. Marianetti and I accompanied him to the Harmon Trophy presentation and drove him to Andrews for his return to Houston. He sent a thoughtful thank you letter and included a small angel trinket he had flown on Apollo 12 for our daughter Jamie.

I am told that during the Apollo 12 overseas tour he tired of the fancy gourmet food being served on the plane and asked about some good ole Italian meals. He was delighted when the Air Force crew obtained a case of Franco American canned spaghetti and meat balls at a Base PX. During the week we spent in New England we ate dinner one night at an Italian restaurant and on two occasions he asked for an extra serving of meatball sauce.

We were now about a year away from the Apollo/Soyuz Test Project (ASTP), the first joint U.S.-Soviet space flight. Three years earlier, May 1972, President Nixon and Soviet Premier Alexei Kosygin, signed an agreement authorizing the joint flight, paving the way for ASTP.

The American crew, using a command module left over from the Apollo program, would be commanded by Gemini and Apollo veteran Tom Stafford; Deke Slayton, one of the Original 7 Mercury astronauts who had been cleared for flight; and Vance Brand, a rookie from the Class of 1966.

It was a personal triumph for Slayton, who had been serving as director of flight crew operations at Houston. In that job Slayton wielded tremendous authority and the responsibility of assigning astronauts to the Apollo flight crews. It was his recommendation that NASA accepted Neil Armstrong as the commander of the historic Apollo 11 lunar mission.

The two-man Soviet crew, using a Soyuz spacecraft, would be commanded by Alexei Leonov, a veteran cosmonaut who was the first human to conduct an EVA in space in 1965. His companion on the flight was cosmonaut Valeri Kubasov.

The flight will be remembered as "the handshake in space" when Stafford and Leonov greeted each other after the successful docking of the two spacecraft. After years of competition between the two nations, ASTP was considered the first step in the improvement of diplomatic relations and is referred to as détente.

I had developed a close working relationship with Stafford after Apollo 10 and during the years (1969-1971), when he temporarily replaced Alan Shepard as chief of the astronaut office after his assignment as Apollo 14 commander. I knew it would be fun working with Stafford again because of his love and support of public affairs. I also knew that Slayton and Brand would follow his lead.

I greatly admired the unsung role that Slayton had played and was delighted that he would, like Shepard before him, at last be given a chance to fly in space. One only has to read his biography not to be impressed. He entered the U.S. Army Air Forces as a cadet in 1942, training as a B-25 Bomber pilot and flying fifty-six combat missions over Europe and later seven combat missions over Japan during World War II.

I remember Deke being asked by an interviewer the significance of his nickname, "Deke". Contrary to the belief it had a religious connotation, he said he acquired the name during his early days in the Air Force and with so many fellow pilots named Donald, he combined the D and K for his middle name Kent, and thus it became "Deke."

The astronauts and cosmonauts worked to become fluent in each other's language and even Tom, with his famous Oklahoma drawl, mastered the difficult Russian language and the others did pretty well also. It helped that the two crews made repeated visits to the others country and benefited from excellent language teachers and classroom instruction.

Following the liftoffs and the meeting and docking in space, the two crews spent forty-six hours in space conducting joint experiments and exchanging gifts and flags and tree seeds, which were returned from space and planted in each others' countries during good will visits by the crews after the flight.

It was shortly after the Apollo splashdown that I began receiving calls from Stafford to discuss a schedule of public appearances. He immediately brought to my attention a proposed trip to the Soviet Union to include spouses and children, which would be followed by a U.S. tour that would include the two cosmonauts and their families.

We also talked about his return to his hometown in Weatherford, Oklahoma, Slayton's hometown in Sparta, Wisconsin and Brand's visit to his hometown in Longmont, Colorado. These would be scheduled after the USSR and American trips were completed. The trip had White House and State Department approval and we began preparations for the trips, which were designed to demonstrate that the then Soviet Union and the U.S. had forged a partnership in science and technological cooperation.

Weather was a determining factor in deciding to visit the USSR first, beginning September 20, and concluding on October 5. The cities and dates were selected by the Russians, who were also responsible for the arrangements, including air, ground travel and lodging.

Special Air Missions at Andrews Air Force Base furnished a VC-135 aircraft to fly the astronaut party and support staff from Andrews to the USSR. Once there, we traveled by USSR-furnished planes and buses to Moscow, Volgograd, Kiev, Sochi, Tbilisi and Novosibirsk, in Siberia.

A highlight of the trip was a visit to Star City, a facility outside Moscow, where the two crews had trained. It was there that they laid a wreath for the late Cosmonaut Yuri Gagarin, the first man to orbit the earth and a beloved hero who died in the crash of his jet in 1967.

The trip was the first of its kind as we dealt with language differences, food and changing weather, where we froze in Siberia but enjoyed balmy weather at Sochi. Following conclusion of the trip, we flew from Moscow to London, where we all boarded commercial flights back to the U.S.

It was a challenging effort moving a group of thirty to forty people at a time from place to place and the collection of baggage from aircraft to buses and to hotels. Stretch and Chuck Biggs, from our Houston Center, did an unbelievable job, especially in the tagging, loading and transporting tons of baggage and never lost a bag in either country.

Before our departure to the USSR, I had been planning the U.S. portion of the trip. With approval of NASA's international relations office and the blessing of the U.S. State Department and the Soviet Embassy, we would begin the trip in Washington on October 13, and fly a chartered military aircraft to Chicago, Omaha, Salt Lake City, San Francisco, with a weekend rest stop in Reno, Nevada. The trip was designed to expose the Soviets to a cross section of America.

The trip would conclude with stops in Los Angeles, Nashville, and Atlanta, New York and back to DC, where the Cosmonaut party would return to the USSR aboard an Aeroflot aircraft. During the visit to Atlanta, the crews visited the memorial to the Reverend Martin Luther King Jr. where they laid a wreath.

The trip to Nashville included a visit to the Country Music Hall of Fame and a Grand Ole Opry performance at Opryland. Among the performers were Roy Acuff, Kitty Wells and Little Jimmy Dickens. The cosmonauts were true country music fans and enjoyed their visit to the Country Music Hall of Fame.

It was amazing for me to compare the two trips and the massive difference in the land mass of the two countries. We had hardly scratched the surface during our two weeks of travel in the Soviet Union. It was one thing to see a country on a map, and quite another to make a real trip through it.

Our group came to realize what the Soviet people had gone through during the war. We saw cities that rose literally from the ashes and the memorials to the more than 20 million people who perished during those years.

Our stay in Washington included a visit with President Ford in the Oval Office. The Soviets reciprocated with a reception hosted by Ambassador Anatoly Dobrynin for the two crews at the then Russian Embassy on 16th Street in DC. It was a lavish affair with Russian vodka and caviar.

In planning the U.S. portion of the tour, I was looking for a weekend rest stop and recommended Las Vegas because of the many great past receptions returning astronaut crews had received there. It was quickly rejected by the Soviets for obvious reasons, but they had no problem when I suggested Reno. It happened that, while we were there, Frank Sinatra was performing, and he offered to host a reception for the group followed by a performance in their honor.

The group left the following morning for Los Angeles, where they were welcomed by workers at the Rockwell International plant at Downey.

The purpose of the visit, like the many made before by returning astronauts flight crews, was to acknowledge and thank the thousands of workers for their efforts in building the many Apollo command and service modules. But on this occasion the astronauts and cosmonauts wanted to express their thanks for the Docking Module, which was designed jointly by the U.S. and Soviet Union and built by Rockwell.

The module enabled a docking between the two spacecraft and served as an airlock between the different atmospheres of the two ships. The module's backup is now on permanent display in the Smithsonian's Air and Space Museum.

That night the group was honored at a pool-side resort hotel reception in Newport Beach hosted by John Wayne. The event, with entertainment by a mariachi band, had a country theme with everyone, including Wayne, wearing western clothing furnished by the Levi Strauss Clothing Company during our earlier stop in San Francisco.

In two nights the ASTP party had been entertained and hosted by two great American Icons, Sinatra—"Ole Blue Eyes"—and Wayne whose many cowboy roles beginning with the 1939 classic, Stagecoach and his Academy Award –winning role in True Grit and earning him the "The Duke" nickname.

Our trip around the U.S. was beginning to wind down, and I was in possession of a photo of me with the three astronauts taken in front of the Washington Hilton Hotel, which they autographed. A smiling Deke handed me the inscribed photo, which read, "To Godfather III, From the Rest of the Family." One thing I will always remember about Deke was his down to Earth demeanor and his favorite description for an astronaut appearance, "A dog and pony show."

Chapter Sixteen

GOODBYE APOLLO... HELLO SPACE SHUTTLE

With the conclusion of the ASTP activities, our public affairs efforts began to focus on the Space Shuttle, which was still six years away from launch. We began our public affairs planning for ALT, the Approach and Landing Tests of the *Enterprise*, which would be used in a series of ground and air tests on the back of a converted 747 at Edwards Air Force Base.

ALT began with the rollout of *Enterprise* at the Rockwell plant in Palmdale, near Edwards Air Force Base with the TV series *Star Trek* creator Gene Rodenberry and many members of the original cast present.

NASA had originally named the orbiter *Constitution* in honor of the U.S. Constitution. However, devoted fans of the *Star Trek* series mounted a write-in letter campaign urging the White House to force NASA to rename the vehicle *Enterprise* after the starship captioned by Captain Kirk in the TV series.

Although Ford did not mention the campaign, he directed NASA to change the name. Fans were later disappointed to learn that *Enterprise* was never designed or built to fly in space. That honor fell to the orbiter *Columbia*.

Following rollout, *Enterprise* began a year-long program in 1977 to test and evaluate the orbiter's aerodynamic flight control systems and subsonic handling characteristics. The tests were conducted by two alternating astronaut crew teams—Fred Haise and Gordon Fullerton, and Joe Engle and Richard Truly. All but Haise later flew in space aboard the shuttle.

Meanwhile, the astronaut corps, which had been well staffed through the years, began to shrink in numbers with the retirement or departure of several of the earlier astronauts.

"Thirty-Five New Guys," The Astronaut Class Of 1978

With the long delay between the conclusion of the Apollo lunar mission in 1972, and the scheduled launch of the Space Shuttle, NASA in January 1978, announced selection of thirty-five astronaut candidates, which included pilots as well as mission specialists for the first time. The first new group of astronauts since 1959 included six women, three male African Americans and a single male Asian American.

From that group came the first American woman (Sally Ride) to fly in space, the first African American (Guion Bluford), the first Jewish-American (Judy Resnik) and Anna Fischer, the first mother in space. The *Challenger* accident on January 28, 1986, would claim the lives of four members of that class.

They included *Challenger's* commander Dick Scobee, Resnik, African-American Ron McNair and Ellison Onizuka, the lone Asian-American. Of course, the flight is remembered because a member of that fatal crew was Christa McAuliffe, making her flight as the first teacher in space.

NASA continued to make selections of astronaut candidates about every two years, and many of the male and female pilots and mission specialists went on to fly aboard Space Shuttle flights until the program was discontinued in 2011.

During that time, five orbiters flew 135 missions involving over 600 astronauts aboard the first reusable spacecraft launched as a rocket, becoming an orbiting spacecraft and landing like an airplane on a runway.

Missions included the deployment of more than fifty satellites for the military, governments, and commercial clients, three interplanetary probes, the Hubble Space Telescope, and perhaps its most important accomplishment was building the International Space Station, which remains in orbit where international crewmembers conduct hundreds of scientific experiments.

The seventh Space Shuttle flight (STS-7), the second mission for the orbiter *Challenger*, was the first featuring a five-member crew that included mission specialist Dr. Sally K. Ride, the first U.S. woman to fly in space in 1983.

She flew one additional flight aboard *Challenger* in 1984, and was scheduled to fly a third mission when the *Challenger* disaster occurred. She joined Neil Armstrong as a member of the Rogers Commission investigating the accident. Later she was assigned to NASA

Headquarters in Washington, where she led a strategic planning effort for America's future in space. In 1987 she left NASA and returned to Stanford University.

A five-year marriage to fellow astronaut Stephen Hawley ended in divorce in 1987, and she died at the age of 61 of pancreatic cancer in July 2012. While she kept her personal life private, it was disclosed after her death that she had maintained a 27-year relationship with a partner, making her the first LGBTQ astronaut.

The Congressional Space Medal of Honor, authorized by Congress in1969 "to recognize any astronaut who in the performance of his duties has distinguished himself by exceptionally meritorious efforts and contributions to the welfare of the Nation and mankind", was about to be awarded for the first time. President Jimmy Carter had decided to make the first presentations on October 1, 1978, the 20th anniversary of NASA's founding.

I felt honored to be asked to provide the names of astronauts I felt were worthy of consideration. My nominations, along with those of several others, were forwarded to the White House by NASA Administrator Dr. Robert Frosch.

I felt my nominations were obvious: Alan Shepard, John Glenn, Neil Armstrong, Frank Borman, Pete Conrad and Gus Grissom, posthumously. I had also submitted the name of Jim Lovell, who did not make the initial list, but was awarded the medal by President Bill Clinton in 1995. As of 2004, all seventeen astronauts killed on a U.S. space mission, are recipients of the prestigious medal and since 2014, twenty-eight have been honored.

Once the White House concurred with the recommendations, we immediately began working on the arrangements for the presentations. Special Air Missions at Andrews (SAM) Air Force Base furnished a special aircraft to fly some of the awardees, spouses and a contingent of NASA and congressional members for the event being staged in the Vehicle Assembly Building (VAB) at the Kennedy Space Center.

It was a logistics challenge coordinating the manifest for the SAM aircraft and President Carter's Air Force One, but it all came together and the ceremony took place as scheduled, with President Carter making the first presentation to Armstrong one of six astronaut recipients, and then the other four. Betty Grissom accepted on behalf of her late husband Gus.

In early 1979, I received word that NASA would provide the thematic exhibit in the U.S. Pavilion at the Paris Air Show. Members of our staff were at work on design of the exhibit, which would feature the Space Shuttle. The orbiter *Columbia* was being prepared for launch, but was delayed because of technical problems at the Rockwell plant in Palmdale, California.

Our participation in the two-week show would include astronauts to help in promoting the shuttle program. It was a perfect opportunity to feature the old and the new. Deke Slayton readily accepted and would be joined by Dr. Rhea Seddon, one of the astronaut candidates selected by NASA in 1978.

A medical doctor, she would represent the new class of astronauts, including six women, African Americans and others of varying disciplines and backgrounds, not just pilots any longer.

It was an experience for me to accompany the two as they appeared at many events and to witness the give and take when asked questions about the roles astronauts would play in the Space Shuttle program. Deke, with his extensive pilot and astronaut background, often found himself disagreeing with some of the views expressed by Seddon, commenting, "She's got a lot to learn." I had to admire the way she stuck to her beliefs refusing to be intimidated by one of the Original 7.

Slayton made no bones that he was there to promote the Space Shuttle and was not hesitant to paste a shuttle patch on windows and other prominent places, including one that got him in trouble with Al Nagy, a NASA Headquarters employee who was the senior representative with the Department of Commerce, responsible for the U.S. participation in the Show.

When Nagy noticed that a shuttle decal was attached to the glass in the French doors of the U.S. Ambassador's residence during a reception, he sought out Slatyon and made the mistake of confronting him in the middle of a crowd, saying, "You embarrassed me and you might as well as had me pull down by pants and slap on a sticker." Slayton, known for responding quickly and effectively said, "Hell Al, if I knew you felt that strongly about it, pull them down and we can do it now."

For me, the Paris Air Show would become a bi-yearly event and I would work with our exhibit people in creating a theme and recommending one or two astronauts to appear for a press conference and participate in air show events and at appearances arranged by the U.S. Information Agency.

We were not sure about astronaut participation for the 1981 air show in early June. We had hoped it would be John Young and Bob Crippen who would hopefully fly *Columbia* before the show began that year.

But a series of technical problems resulted in delays and it wasn't until April 12 that the historic launch occurred and a successful landing two days later on April 14 at Edwards Air Force Base.

We were now assured that they would be available for the opening of the air show. After debriefings and a news conference, we accepted an early invitation from Roone Arledge, President of ABC News, who wanted Young and Crippen to address a meeting of ABC-TV executives at a meeting aboard the historic *Queen Mary*, docked at Long Beach, California.

It was while there we accepted a personal invitation to see the huge wooden flying boat, the Hughes H-4 Hercules dubbed the "Spruce Goose," built by Howard Hughes. The controversial craft had been stored for years in a special environmentally-controlled hangar at Long Beach, and was about to be moved after Hughes death to a new location.

It ranks as one of the big thrills of my life to see the plane and sit in the same seat as Howard Hughes when he piloted the massive plane on its only flight, which lasted about a minute over Long Beach Harbor on November 2, 1947.

Young and Crippen addressed the ABC executives following presentation of a brief video of their flight. After an overnight stay aboard the *Queen Mary*, we departed for Chicago and a traditional welcome by Mayor Daley and then returned to Houston.

A trip to Washington followed and the usual appearances at the White House and Capitol Hill. Rockwell International hosted a reception at the Blair House, and the guest list included members of congress, the diplomatic corps and many other dignitaries.

A reception at the Anacostia Navy Yard, involving now Vice President George H.W. Bush followed. The astronauts and wives arrived late and we were escorted to the speaker's stage ahead of many waiting Navy admirals and high ranking officials. I recall Crippen, a U.S. Navy Captain, saying, "Thanks Gene. You just ended any chance of a future Navy promotion."

Young and Crippen had already agreed to participate at the Paris Air Show in June, but they first had to complete appearances in South Carolina, Salt Lake City, San Francisco and New York. They were honored at commencement at the University of South Carolina in Columbia, where they, along with composer John Williams, received honorary degrees.

The trip to Salt Lake City had political implications, which involved Utah Senator Jake Garn. Garn, a powerful member of a committee that controlled NASA funds and who a few years later flew aboard the Space Shuttle. He had arranged for the world-famous Mormon Tabernacle Choir to present a special concert in honor of the first shuttle flight.

It was especially controversial because of the separation of church and state, but NASA felt compelled to honor the request and the Senator had gone to great lengths to arrange the special concert in the Mormon Tabernacle.

The choir was in the midst of an overseas tour, and the special concert honoring the *Columbia* flight would require a change in scheduling and their charter flight diverted back to Salt Lake City. During the flight, the Choir practiced the words to the song, "Columbia, the Gem of the Ocean," which was the highlight of the concert, along with other religious and patriotic songs.

Prior to the concert, Young and Crippen had spent a hectic day participating in thirteen events in Ogden and Salt Lake City, which included a press conference, luncheon speech and narration of a video from their flight, which they narrated before the choir's presentation.

Our trip to San Francisco included an appearance before the Word Affairs Council, where Young and the Apollo 16 crew had appeared nine years earlier. Our visit there this time involved then Mayor Diane Feinstein, who was later to become a U.S. Senator, and Shirley Temple Black, the child movie star who had served as a U.S. ambassador to Ghana and chief of protocol at the State Department under President Reagan.

We had a free evening and thanks to the mayor's office, were invited to a dinner theater at the famous Mark Hopkins Hotel and a performance by Ella Fitzgerald, who introduced the astronauts. Following her performance, we were invited back stage to meet her and the crew presented her a photo of *Columbia*'s landing with the inscription, "To Ella Fitzgerald, the first lady of song" with the best wishes of the STS 1Crew. I was just proud to be there and the opportunity to meet a songstress I had long admired.

The trip to New York was well along in the planning. Governor Hugh Carey and Mayor Ed Koch would host a state dinner and the

Slayton and Leonov during the ASTP Mission

Stafford and Leonov at an anniversary event in 2015

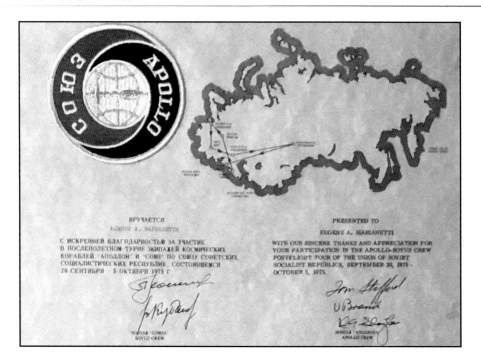

ВРУЧАЕТСЯ

ЕВГЕНИ А. МАРИАНЕТТИ

С ИСКРЕННЕЙ БЛАГОДАРНОСТЬЮ ЗА УЧАСТИЕ
В ПОСЛЕПОЛЕТНОМ ТУРНЕ ЭКИПАЖЕЙ КОСМИЧЕСКИХ
КОРАБЛЕЙ "АПОЛЛОН" И "СОЮЗ" ПО СОЮЗУ СОВЕТСКИХ
СОЦИАЛИСТИЧЕСКИХ РЕСПУБЛИК, СОСТОЯВШЕМСЯ
20 СЕНТЯБРЯ - 5 ОКТЯБРЯ 1975 Г.

ЭКИПАЖ "СОЮЗА"
SOYUZ CREW

PRESENTED TO

EUGENE A. MARIANETTI

WITH OUR SINCERE THANKS AND APPRECIATION FOR
YOUR PARTICIPATION IN THE APOLLO-SOYUZ CREW
POSTFLIGHT TOUR OF THE UNION OF SOVIET
SOCIALIST REPUBLICS, SEPTEMBER 20, 1975 -
OCTOBER 5, 1975.

ЭКИПАЖ "АПОЛЛОНА"
APOLLO CREW

PRESENTED TO

EUGENE A. MARIANETTI

WITH OUR SINCERE THANKS AND APPRECIATION FOR
YOUR PARTICIPATION IN THE APOLLO-SOYUZ CREW
POSTFLIGHT TOUR OF THE UNITED STATES,
OCTOBER 13, 1975 - OCTOBER 25, 1975.

APOLLO CREW
ЭКИПАЖ "АПОЛЛОНА"

ВРУЧАЕТСЯ

ЕВГЕНИ А. МАРИАНЕТТИ

С ИСКРЕННЕЙ БЛАГОДАРНОСТЬЮ ЗА УЧАСТИЕ В
ПОСЛЕПОЛЕТНОМ ТУРНЕ ЭКИПАЖЕЙ КОСМИЧЕСКИХ
КОРАБЛЕЙ "АПОЛЛОН" И "СОЮЗ" ПО
СОЕДИНЕННЫМ ШТАТАМ АМЕРИКИ,
СОСТОЯВШЕМСЯ 13-25 ОКТЯБРЯ 1975 Г.

SOYUZ CREW
ЭКИПАЖ "СОЮЗА"

The author sitting in the same seat where Howard Hughes sat years earlier in the brief flight of the Spruce Goose in 1947.

Armstrong and Aldrin planting the U.S. flag on the lunar surface. This scene was not featured in the recent movie "First Man", which was based on the book by James R. Hansen.

179

The author looks in awe in the suite of Jean MacArthur, widow of Army General Douglas MacArthur.

The author (standing) review the upcoming schedule with John Young and his wife, Suzy, while on board a NASA jet for an event in Chicago, 1972.

EUGENE A. CERNAN
900 TOWN & COUNTRY LANE   SUITE 300   HOUSTON, TEXAS 77024   (713) 827-9922

April 28, 1994

Mr. Gene Marianetti
NASA Headquarters
Washington, D.C.

Dear Geno:

Congratulations on your "retirement"--just another
word for moving on to bigger and better things.

I could not agree with you more that this is the
time--things have changed, haven't they? Nevertheless
you will be missed and your contributions to history
and your country not forgotten.

Wishing you "fair winds and following seas as you
take your own Giant Leap...."

Letter to follow, but in the meantime, let's just
reflect on some of the fun times we had together!
"Around the world ♩♪♪ in '73!"

Love to Peg.

Sincerely,

Eugene A. Cernan

EAC/cdj

Gene Cernan's letter on the author's retirement from NASA in 1994.

Neil Armstrong and Gene Cernan...the first and last astronauts to walk on the Moon.

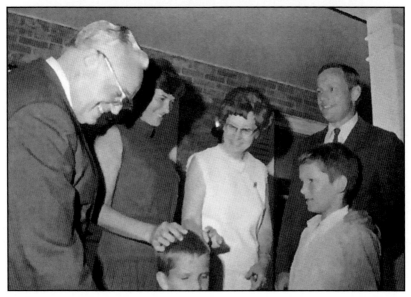

Neil Armstrong family photo on arrival in Wapakoneta for a hometown welcome. Pictured l-r: Father Stephen Armstrong, wife Janet, mother Viola, Neil, and the Armstrong boys Mark and Rick.

182

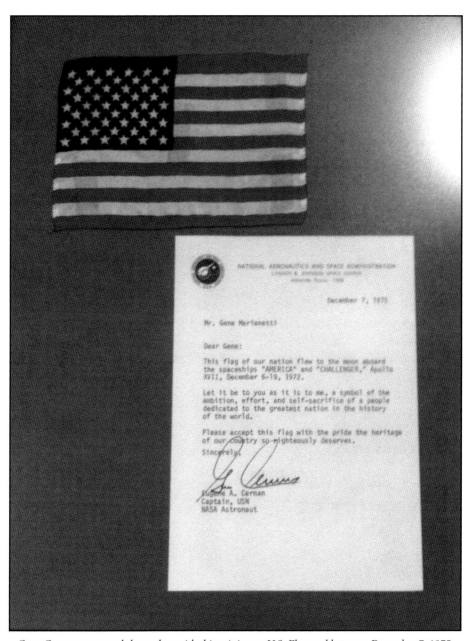

Gene Cernan presented the author with this miniature U.S. Flag and letter on December 7, 1975.

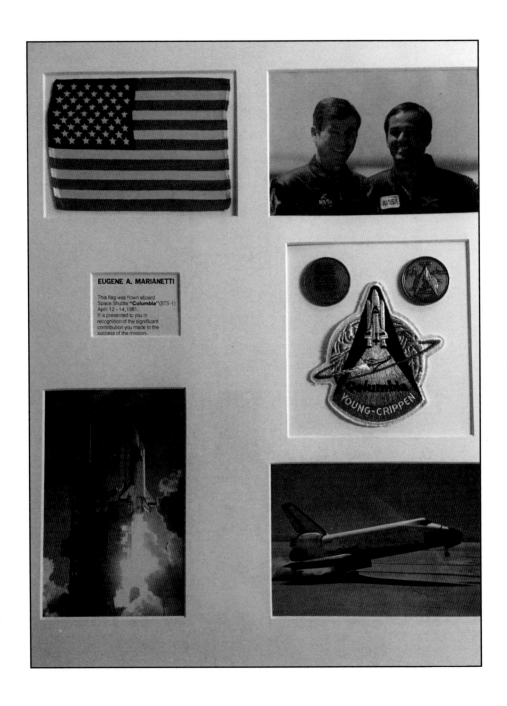

EUGENE A. MARIANETTI

This flag was flown aboard
Space Shuttle **"Columbia"** (STS-1)
April 12 - 14, 1981.
It is presented to you in
recognition of the significant
contribution you made to the
success of the mission.

Gene Cernan and his daughter, Tracy.

Apollo 17 astronaut Ron Evans and John Glenn, to his left, exchange greetings with Walter Cronkite at a State Dinner honoring the Apollo 11 crew on August 13, 1969.

Crew of the Space Shuttle Challenger

Day of Remembrance ceremony at Arlington National Cemetery

Gerry Griffin presents the author with a Performance Award in 1981.

George H.W. Bush (center) with Mrs. Douglas MacArthur

Jack King, the Kennedy Space Center public information officer and launch countdown commentator stationed in Launch Control for Apollo 11.

The author joined the Apollo 11 crew at a 20th Anniversary event at the Air and Space Museum. The author is shown updating Neil Armstrong on the status of the United Airlines crash earlier that day. The crew discussed the possibility of cancelling the observance in recognition of the tragedy, but in the end went ahead with the program.

John Young meets Igor Sikorsky during an Apollo 16 tour in Connecticut. Sikorsky was an aviation legend who pioneered the development of the helicopter and fixed-wing aircraft.

Burial at Sea for Neil Armstrong

When moving across the country, the Space Shuttle was always flown atop the Shuttle Carrier Aircraft (SCA), a modified Boeing 747

The XV15 NASA Tilt Rotor at the Paris Air Show, 1981.

Author Gene Marianetti behind his desk at NASA headquarters in Washington, D.C.

Astronauts of Apollo 12 served as the Grand Marshals of the 81st Tournament of Roses Parade in Pasadena, California, January 1, 1970.

Neil Armstrong addressing a joint session of Congress, September 16, 1969.

NEIL A. ARMSTRONG
P.O. BOX 436
LEBANON, OH 45036

April 25, 1994

Mr. Eugene Marianetti
Chief, Special Events Branch
NASA
Washington, D. C. 20546

Dear Gene:

Hearty congratulations on the occasion of your graduation
from NASA. Yours has been an outstanding career in a historic
time and many of us are in your debt for the extensive help
you have provided. Your thoughtfulness and sensitivity have
been very important to us and have benefitted NASA in more
ways than they will ever know.

I hope that you will enjoy your post-NASA days as much as I
have. There is a great deal going on in the outside world,
and I believe you will discover a new perspective that you
will find satisfying.

I hope our paths cross often.

All the best.

Sincerely,

Neil

Neil A. Armstrong

NAA:vw

Alabama Governor George Wallace and wife, Cornelia, welcome the Skylab 2 crew to the Executive Mansion in Montgomery, 1973. Pictured are Joe Kerwin, Paul Weitz, and Pete Conrad, with the author in back.

The author with Neil Armstrong (at right) during an event celebrating the 5th Anniversary of the Apollo 11 launch, Cocoa Beach, Florida, July 16, 1974.

The author with Buzz Aldrin (at right) during an event celebrating the 5th Anniversary of the Apollo 11 launch, Cocoa Beach, Florida, July 16, 1974.

NASA staffers Chuck Biggs and Stretch Flanagan unfold the Apollo/Soyuz flag on arrival in Moscow, September 28, 1975. to begin a two-week tour of the then Soviet Union. With them behind the flag are Alexei Leonov (wearing hat) and the author.

The Space Shuttle program began with the rollout of the orbiter Enterprise *at the Rockwell facility in Palmdale, California on September 17, 1976. Pictured with NASA Administrator James Fletcher are Gene Rodenberry, creator of the TV series "Star Trek", along with actors Leonard Nimoy (Dr. Spock), Nichelle Nichols (Lt. Uhura), DeForest Kelly (Bones McCoy), George Takei (Mr. Sulu), and Walter Koenig (Mr. Chekov). The author, who had planned the rollout ceremony, is pictured to the right with his hand in the air.*

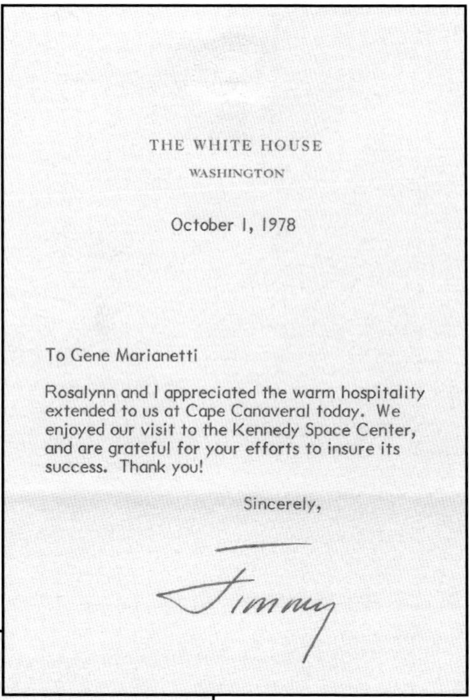

Thank you letter from President Jimmy Carter for the first Congressional Space Medal of Honor ceremony at Kennedy Space Center, October 1, 1978.

THE WHITE HOUSE

WASHINGTON

October 1, 1978

To Gene Marianetti

Rosalynn and I appreciated the warm hospitality extended to us at Cape Canaveral today. We enjoyed our visit to the Kennedy Space Center, and are grateful for your efforts to insure its success. Thank you!

Sincerely,

Jimmy

First Presentation of
The Congressional Space Medal of Honor
by the President of the United States

National Aeronautics and
Space Administration
John F. Kennedy Space Center
October First, 1978

Program for the First Presentation of the Congressional Space Medal of Honor signed by astronauts Neil A. Armstrong, Frank Borman, Charles Conrad Jr., John H. Glenn Jr., and Alan B. Shepard, and Betty Grissom, wife of Virgil I. Grissom, October 1, 1978.

The author with Neil Armstrong during the 10th Anniversary of Apollo 11, July 19, 1979.

NASA Administrator James Beggs presents the author with his second Exceptional Service Award (ESM), which recognized his successful planning, implementation and management of the Paris Air Show, 20th Anniversary activities for Apollo 11, and the reestablished, more effective guest operations for Space Shuttle launches and landings, September 15, 1981. In his career, Marianetti received three ESMs.

Astronauts John Young and Robert Crippen, who flew the Space Shuttle Columbia's *first space flight in April 1981.*

The author represented NASA in the presentation of a special award to Senator Barry Goldwater (R-AZ) in recognition of his support of NASA and the advancement of space and aeronautics. The presentation was made during the annual Iron Gate Chapter banquet by the Air Force Association in New York City.

The recent death of former President H.W. Bush brought to mind the several times the Apollo 13, 14, 15 and 16 crews met with him during the years (1971-1973) he served as the U.S. Ambassador to the United Nations in New York. Here, Apollo 15 commander Dave Scott and command service module pilot Al Worden make a presentation to him during their visit to UN Headquarters in July 1971. Lunar module pilot Jim Irwin is to the right of Mr. Bush. The author is seen behind the left shoulder of President Bush.

201

The author escorts Senior NASA Pilot Joe Algranti at the Paris Air Show, June 1983. Algranti had just landed the plane carrying the Space Shuttle Enterprise *to the show.*

Astronaut Rick Hauck and NASA Administrator Dick Truly present the author with the "Silver Snoopy Award" for his efforts during the Space Shuttle Transportation System Program, January 26, 1989.

Cocktail napkin from Air Force One.

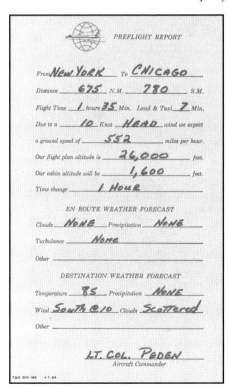

PREFLIGHT REPORT

From **NEW YORK** To **CHICAGO**

Distance **675** N.M. **780** S.M.

Flight Time **1** hours **35** Min. Land & Taxi **7** Min.

Due to a **10** Knot **HEAD** wind we expect

a ground speed of **552** miles per hour.

Our flight plan altitude is **26,000** feet.

Our cabin altitude will be **1,600** feet.

Time change **1 HOUR**

EN ROUTE WEATHER FORECAST

Clouds **NONE** Precipitation **NONE**

Turbulance **None**

Other _____

DESTINATION WEATHER FORECAST

Temperature **85** Precipitation **NONE**

Wind **South @ 10** Clouds **Scattered**

Other _____

LT. COL. PEDEN
Aircraft Commander

TSR 300-186   4-7-64

Aboard the Presidential Aircraft

Preflight report given to passengers of Air Force One.

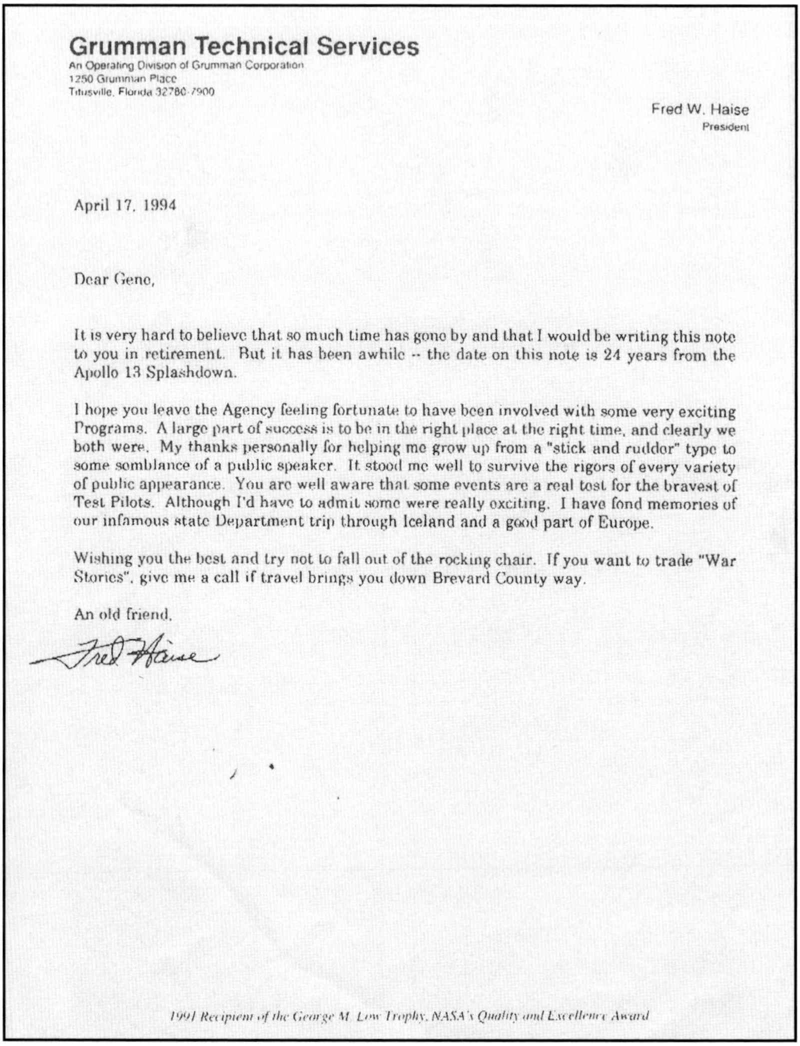

Grumman Technical Services
An Operating Division of Grumman Corporation
1250 Grumman Place
Titusville, Florida 32780-7900

Fred W. Haise
President

April 17, 1994

Dear Gene,

It is very hard to believe that so much time has gone by and that I would be writing this note to you in retirement. But it has been awhile -- the date on this note is 24 years from the Apollo 13 Splashdown.

I hope you leave the Agency feeling fortunate to have been involved with some very exciting Programs. A large part of success is to be in the right place at the right time, and clearly we both were. My thanks personally for helping me grow up from a "stick and rudder" type to some semblance of a public speaker. It stood me well to survive the rigors of every variety of public appearance. You are well aware that some events are a real test for the bravest of Test Pilots. Although I'd have to admit some were really exciting. I have fond memories of our infamous state Department trip through Iceland and a good part of Europe.

Wishing you the best and try not to fall out of the rocking chair. If you want to trade "War Stories", give me a call if travel brings you down Brevard County way.

An old friend,

Fred Haise

1991 Recipient of the George M. Low Trophy, NASA's Quality and Excellence Award

Letter from astronaut Fred W. Haise upon the author's retirement from NASA.

Apollo 11 astronauts Neil Armstrong, Buzz Aldrin and Michael Collins stand by the Columbia *at the National Air and Space Museum, 1979.*

The author (left) with Deke Slayton, one of the Original 7 Mercury astronauts, at the 1979 Paris Air Show. To the right is space journalist Jacques Tiziou.

Dr. Sally Ride with the author and his wife, Peg, at the home of the late Al Neuharth, founder of USA Today in Cocoa Beach, Florida, following the Space Shuttle launch, 1985.

Pictured l-r: the author, NASA PAO Dave Garrett, Dick Rutan, and Jeana Yeager, June 1987. Rutan and Yeager piloted the first non-stop, non-refueled flight around the world in the Rutan Voyager aircraft from December 14-23, 1986.

NEIL A. ARMSTRONG
P.O. BOX 436
LEBANON, OH 45036

February 20, 1989

Mr. E. A. Marianetti
National Aeronautics and Space Administration
Mail Code LPE
Washington, D. C. 20546

Dear Gene:

I have been receiving many inquiries, but have not yet made
commitments.

I expect to be attending a meeting in Paris on June 5-7, and
will plan to stay over for the US Pavilion opening on June 9.
I can't think of anything that I could contribute to a press
conference, but will listen to any reasons that might exist.

I expect to have transportation over but would appreciate
NASA providing a return. I would expect to return to the US
as soon after the pavilion opening as practical.

With regard to the U.S. celebrations, I have frequently
stated a preference for a single NASA event that would
involve the entire Apollo program, with involvement by
project personnel and flight crews from all flights. Although
I don't know the details, I understand the Houston planning
may have some of this.

To expect the A-11 crew to attend all the events over a
week-long marathon seems a bit much. Perhaps we could split
up some of the coverage. My own preferences are (1) JSC and
(2) KSC.

I don't know how Mike and Buzz feel about the overall effort,
but will solicit their opinions. Gene, you've done a good job
in coordinating all of this, and I have told you that I
support the outline you developed. I do hope we can continue
to improve on it.

Sincerely,

Neil A. Armstrong

RECEIVED

NAA:vw
cc: Aldrin & Collins

David R. Scott
1300 B MANHATTAN AVENUE • MANHATTAN BEACH, CALIFORNIA 90266

May 3, 1994

Gene:

As you embark on a new journey, please accept
our gratitude for your leadership, your patience,
and, especially, your superior and consistent performance
during our many journeys for Apollo —
The pleasant memories of our travels together
are indelible in the adventures of the Times. !

Dave

*Letter from David R. Scott congratulating the author upon his retirement
from NASA, May 3, 1994.*

207

NATIONAL AERONAUTICS AND SPACE ADMINISTRATION
LYNDON B. JOHNSON SPACE CENTER
HOUSTON, TEXAS 77058

REPLY TO
ATTN OF: PA-EAC-74-233

NOV 8 1974

Mr. John P. Donnelly
Assistant Administrator for Public Affairs
National Aeronautics and Space Administration
Washington, D. C. 20546

Dear John:

This letter is offered as a word of commendation for the total
and complete support I received from Mr. Eugene A. Marianetti
on my recent visit to Yugoslavia, Romania, and Czechoslovakia.
It was not an easy trip to prepare for because of the short notice,
lack of confirmed itineraries, and my personal absence on ASTP
negotiations in Moscow. It was most difficult in real time because of the political environments and the sensitivity to prevailing
situations of which we both had to stay knowledgeable.

Gene dedicated himself both personally and professionally to
making this trip a success and following through with the extended
paperwork after its completeness. He was more than simply
staff support or an asset--he was a necessity.

The worthwhile accomplishments of this recent Eastern European
trip can be contributed directly to Gene. He lived by the creed
"if its worth doing--its worth doing well." And I add that it
could not have been done without him.

Please pass a well done and a thank you on to Mr. Eugene A.
Marianetti.

Sincerely,

Eugene A. Cernan
Captain, USN
NASA Astronaut

cc:
AC/G. W. S. Abbey
AE/H. E. Clements
FGA/E. A. Marianetti

*Letter of commendation by Captain Eugene Cernan for the author's role in coordinating
Cernan's trip to Eastern Europe, November 8, 1974.*

astronauts would then depart for Paris the next day. However, a phone call from New York promoter Len Silverfine before our arrival raised some interesting possibilities.

Silverfine was sponsoring "The Great American Flag" project and was asking that Young and Crippen attend the unfolding of the huge (366 by 193) foot American Flag in Central Park. Our commitments in Paris would preclude accepting his invitation.

He then suggested providing complimentary tickets for the five of us to fly the French Concorde from JFK to Paris, which would cut the seven hour flight time nearly in half and get us to Paris in time to meet our schedule there.

The chance to fly aboard the Concorde was an offer Young and Crippen could not pass up. However, I needed approval by NASA management because regulations required that government employees fly only aboard American carriers unless extenuating circumstances were involved.

Plans were in place for the astronauts to attend an early lunch, which would be followed by the Great American Flag unfolding. But like the Barbra Streisand song "Don't Rain on My Parade," a steady rain forced a postponement of the event, which was later held on June 18 in Central Park, with a performance by Simon and Garfunkel.

Unable to participate in the Flag ceremony, we left the luncheon and departed for JFK and boarded the Concorde at 2:45 that afternoon (8:45 P.M. Paris time). Flying at Mach 2.04 at 1,350 miles an hour at 60,000 feet at twice the speed of sound was an unforgettable experiences.

The Concorde seating was considered all first class with a single narrow aisle, with two seats on either side. A Mach speedometer kept us aware of our air speed and once into the flight the captain invited us to the cockpit, which was quite an experience.

Also aboard and drawing considerable attention, was actor Paul Newman. He was very gracious when introduced to our group. I found flying aboard the Concorde fascinating, and it only took three hours and thirty minutes before we touched down at Charles De Gaulle Airport about midnight Paris time.

The astronauts were guests at the residence of the U.S. Ambassador and enjoyed the VIP quarters. Security was of great concern, and the Embassy was working closely with French officials who provided around-the -clock security for the astronauts. The assassination of

John Lennon the previous December and the attempted assassination of Pope John Paul II a month earlier raised concern for their safety.

While the astronauts were hailed and toasted for the success of the first shuttle flight, the real crowd pleaser was a NASA research aircraft that had been flown to Paris from California. The Bell XV-15 Tilt rotor, a vertical takeoff and landing experimental aircraft, performed daily. The *New York Times* praised its performances, writing, "And if ever there was a lovable plane, it is the Bell XV-15, the hit of the show performed a series of maneuvers including bowing to the crowd."

As our time in Paris ended, I flew with John and Suzy to London, where he would be inducted as a member of the British Royal Aeronautical Society. It was then on to Madrid, Spain, where John visited the NASA tracking station a few miles outside of Madrid.

The station had functioned since the early days of the space program and was a vital piece of the agency's worldwide deep space tracking network. He was there representing the astronaut office and thanked the workers for their dedicated efforts.

The U.S. Information Agency had arranged a separate schedule for Crippen and his wife, and he left Paris accompanied by our PAO Officer Debbie Rahn for stops in several European cities before returning home.

We had observed the tenth anniversary of the first lunar landing two years earlier in 1979, which featured a free evening on July 19 at the Washington Hilton, which furnished a private room with beverages and finger foods for the three astronauts and their wives and the chance to mix and chat freely with staff members who had accompanied them on the 45-day around the world trip in 1969. The next day the astronauts participated in numerous media events and news conference and a reception that evening in the Air and Space Museum.

The 15th anniversary occurred while NASA was participating at the 1984 Louisiana World Exposition in New Orleans. The orbiter *Enterprise* was on display in the U.S. Pavilion and the three astronauts, accompanied by Administrator James Beggs, attended a small dinner with Dr. Rocco Petrone serving as the master of ceremonies. He had been the director of Apollo launch operations at the Kennedy Space Center and served as director of the Marshall Space Flight Center in Alabama.

That evening the party was treated to a ride aboard a real paddle-boat on a Mississippi River cruise, with entertainment by a Dixieland Band. It was truly an enjoyable evening free from autograph seekers and the chance to sit back and enjoy the cruise. Guests received a specially designed presentation item to mark the occasion.

A year earlier in 1983, *Enterprise*, despite much consternation within NASA, would be flown on the back of the 747 Shuttle Carrier Aircraft from its base in California, to the Paris Air Show. Officials were concerned that the 747 was "a single point failure" and represented the only means of transporting orbiters from California landings back to Florida for re-launchings.

This was prior to the purchase by NASA of a second 747 for a backup capability. After many high level meetings between NASA management and security officials, it was decided to make the necessary arrangements with emphasis on security, to fly the pair to the Paris Air Show in June.

As an opportunity to expose the program to worldwide attention, it was decided to expand the trip and add stops in Germany, Italy, England and Canada, with a final promotional landing and display at Dulles International Airport in Virginia outside Washington.

The multi-country trip was a huge success and tennis star John McEnroe is remembered in a photo taken during the French Open, when he interrupted a serve to briefly gaze in amazement as the SCA and *Enterprise* flew overhead.

The stop at Dulles for a weekend of free public viewing required many coordination meetings between NASA, state, local, Dulles and law enforcement representatives. The event was widely publicized, and motorists and thousands of others watched on a Friday from the Beltway and other locations as the SCA and *Enterprise* flew over the Potomac River and touched down at Dulles were it was towed to a reserved viewing area.

While no official count was kept, it is believed that thousands drove to Dulles that weekend to see up close the *Enterprise* mounted atop the SCA. The *Enterprise* was then flown back to Edwards, where it remained until being transferred to the Smithsonian's Air and Space Museum.

It finally went on public display in December 2003 at the NASM Udvar-Hazy Space Center in Fairfax, Virginia, until replaced by the veteran shuttle orbiter *Discovery*. *Enterprise* was then transported to

New York, where it has been on display at the *Intrepid* Sea, Air and Space Museum Complex since 2012.

NASA again furnished the thematic exhibit for the 1985 Paris Air Show, with participation by astronauts from earlier Space Shuttle flights and a display of aeronautical and space exhibits.

Successful flights of the Space Shuttle were becoming routine, but on January 28, 1986, the Space Shuttle *Challenger*, with a crew of seven, blew up 73 seconds after launch, killing five NASA astronauts and two mission specialists including Christa McAuliffe, a school teacher from Concord, New Hampshire, who had been selected from thousands of applicants to become the first in the Teacher in Space Program.

Several factors may have influenced the tragedy. James Beggs who was appointed NASA Administrator in 1981 by President Reagan, had taken an indefinite leave of absence after a federal grand jury indicted him and others for fraud in December 1985.

The charges stemmed from when Beggs was an executive with General Dynamics. The indictment was later dismissed and prompted an apology from Attorney General Ed Meese saying the charges should never have been filed. While it has been recognized as a mistake, it is believed to have caused irreparable damage to the space program.

With Beggs on indefinite leave, Deputy Administrator Dr. Bill Graham became acting administrator. Graham had been nominated by President Reagan, but Beggs opposed the nomination, saying Graham was not qualified and lobbied the White House and members of Congress to reject it. However, Graham won confirmation and settled in as the agency's number two man.

Graham as acting administrator flew to Florida for the teacher in space launch, which had originally been scheduled for Sunday, January 26. But for the first time in the history of the space program, a scheduled launch was delayed based on a weather forecast.

A strong moving weather pattern was expected to arrive in Florida about launch time, but we awoke to a beautiful morning with bright sunshine and ideal launch conditions. It was then we learned that the weather front had stalled in Tennessee.

A series of technical glitches followed, which forced further postponements and a cold front finally arrived on Tuesday, January 28, raising doubts that the launch would occur.

By now Graham and others like me had left Florida on Sunday and were back in Washington watching the countdown activities on TV, and could not believe when the decision was made to launch despite TV coverage showing the formation of ice on the launch tower and freezing temperatures. Of course, it was a normal liftoff and we could not believe the explosion, which occurred 73 seconds later just after the command from mission control to the crew "Go at Throttle Up."

Under normal conditions, Beggs would have been in the launch control center, and many felt he would never have given the okay for launch based on the freezing weather conditions. It was later determined that the accident was caused by an O rings failure in one of the solid rocket boosters and that the freezing temperatures greatly contributed to the explosion.

For NASA public affairs it became a chaotic situation, and we quickly learned to deal with a tragedy witnessed by thousands in person and on live TV. A grieving public responded with phone calls and thousands of letters, telegrams and other expressions of sympathy. Each day the U.S. Postal Service was making scheduled and unscheduled deliveries of duffel bags of mail from a grieving public.

The disaster resulted in a thirty-two month hiatus in the shuttle program and formation of the Rogers Commission by President Reagan to investigate the accident. Neil Armstrong, as the first man on the Moon and Dr. Sally Ride, the first American woman to fly in space, were named to the commission.

Our office developed response letters, but it soon became apparent that we would need outside assistance, and NASA management authorized us to hire a correspondence contractor to use our responses and send letter acknowledgements.

Some of the letters we received contained money and the desire to help with the funding of a new orbiter to replace *Challenger*. By law, NASA transferred the funds, which eventually totaled more than $100,000 to the U. S. Treasury Department.

A shuttle replacement was eventually authorized and funded by Congress and named *Endeavour*. Its first flight in May 1992, was about five years after the loss of *Challenger*. Of course we had no way of knowing history would repeat itself when we lost the first Space Shuttle *Columbia* and the seven member crew on February 1, 2003, during reentry following its 28th mission in space.

Our theme for the 1987 Paris Air Show focused on "The Return to Flight," and featured a short video narrated by actor Burgess Meredith. The video played at intervals and was part of the NASA presence, which featured static aeronautics and space exhibits.

NASA officials attended and provided a status update on the investigation into the *Challenger* accident while awaiting results from the Rogers Commission and the internal investigations being conducted by NASA and its contractors.

We welcomed a number of special guests to the NASA exhibit including Dick Rutan and Jeana Yeager. They became the first people to circumnavigate the world without refueling their unique *Voyager* airplane.

They had departed from Edwards Air Force Base in California on December 14, 1986 in *Voyager* and flew non-stop, landing back at Edwards on December 23, 24,986 miles later. The historic aircraft now hangs in the National Air and Space Museum in Washington, D.C.

It was a year after the *Challenger* disaster that NASA began a yearly tradition of observing January 25 of each year "A Day of Remembrance" to recognize the crews of Apollo 1, the Space Shuttle *Challenger* and later *Columbia* and its seven member crew on February 1, 2003, as well as other colleagues who lost their lives while furthering the cause of space exploration and discovery.

Still observed in 2019, NASA's Day of Remembrance, usually held on January 31st each year, was rescheduled because of the partial government shutdown and held at Arlington National Cemetery on February 7th, with Vice President Mike Pence and NASA Administrator James Bridenstine in attendance.

The day includes an observance and wreath-laying ceremonies at the *Challenger* and *Columbia* Memorial sites at Arlington National Cemetery in Virginia, and a commemoration at the Astronaut Memorial at the Kennedy Space Center involving family and friends of the astronauts.

In early 1989, we began to plan for the 20th anniversary of the first lunar landing. It began with a call to Armstrong, who agreed to an observance but expressed hope that he and the others would do individual appearances rather than appear as a crew, especially since this observance would be far more extensive involving more places and events than those held previously.

After receiving approval from Collins and Aldrin, we agreed to a meeting/briefing at NASA Headquarters for NASA Administrator Vice Admiral Richard Truly, who joined the astronaut corps in 1969 and flew two Space Shuttle missions before leaving NASA, and returning to the Navy where he accepted the command of the U.S. Navy Space Command at Dahlgren, Virginia.

He returned to assist NASA with the return to flight after the *Challenger* accident, and was eventually named Administrator by President George H.W. Bush. Armstrong, speaking on behalf of the crew again argued for individual, rather than crew, appearances and, in effect, splitting up the workload. It was finally decided that the three would appear in public as they had in space as a crew.

Our public affairs staff in Washington had prepared an anniversary press kit to be distributed in advance of the anniversary, so that the media would have adequate time to prepare articles and stories related to the event. Our graphics department developed a commemorative anniversary patch for the event. The crew agreed to meet in Washington on Friday, May 26, where they underwent extensive questioning from the major TV networks and major daily newspapers.

I had planned a week-long observance that would involve stops in Huntsville, Alabama, Kennedy Space Center, Florida, Washington, D.C., and concluding with appearances at the Johnson Space Center in Houston. The Washington stop would include U.S. Senate and House receptions and a barbecue hosted by President and Mrs. George H.W. Bush on the White House lawn on the July 20 anniversary date.

But, we first wanted to feature the astronauts at the Paris Air Show at LeBourget, which was scheduled for early June. It would mean a split observance with nearly a month in between. Neil was the first to agree and Mike and Buzz followed suit.

The three astronauts and their spouses flew to Paris for three days and participated in the opening of the NASA exhibit at the entrance to the U. S. Pavilion. Truly delivered an opening statement and then introduced the three astronauts, who responded with brief remarks.

Later in the day, they were again introduced by Truly at a news conference in the Pavilion, and concluded their participation by attending the traditional NASA reception held in the exhibit area, which featured a scale model of the Hubble Space Telescope which was scheduled for launch in 1990.

Following a reception in the NASA exhibit area, the astronauts departed for the U.S. and a nearly month's break before participating in a week-long series of events in Alabama, Florida, Washington and Houston.

The first event to mark the occasion was a a huge outdoor space-flight inspired light and sound event planned and organized by author/ lecturer and founder of Space Camp Ed Buckbee. The program recognized the role of the Marshall Space Flight Center in Huntsville, along with Director Dr. Wernher von Braun and his team of rocket experts who were responsible for the development of the family of Saturn rockets used in the Apollo program. A reception followed at the Alabama Space and Rocket Center.

Following an overnight stay, the group flew aboard a NASA jet to Cape Canaveral on July 16, where they were transported to a stage near the Vehicle Assembly Building and introduced to a crowd of thousands bused to the affair for what was an almost repeat of the ceremony marking the fifth Apollo 11 anniversary in 1974.

After introductions, followed by brief remarks by the three astronauts, the recorded countdown of their launch was played and coincided with the exact moment of liftoff, 9:32 a.m. on July 16, 1969. After the ceremony, the astronauts were driven in vintage Corvettes to Cocoa Beach, where they were honored at a Brevard County civic luncheon.

Four days later, the 20th anniversary activities resumed in the main lobby of the National Air and Space Museum, where the U.S. Postal Service dedicated the first day of issuance of a Priority Mail Service Stamp. Its designer, Christopher Calle, is the son of Paul Calle, the veteran illustrator who produced the 1969 First Man on the Moon airmail stamp.

Postmaster General Anthony Frank unveiled the stamp much the same way one of his predecessors Malcolm Blount had done 20 years earlier. His dedication was followed by remarks by Truly, who then introduced the astronauts and Vice President Dan Quayle, who introduced President George H.W. Bush.

President and Mrs. Bush then hosted an invitation only barbeque on the south lawn of the White House. I was fortunate to receive an invitation, and the event concluded with a photo session featuring the astronauts and their wives with the President and First Lady. A real treat for all was the unexpected arrival of "Mille", Mrs. Bush's famous spaniel.

Before our departure from the barbecue, President Bush invited the astronauts and their wives to accompany him and Mrs. Bush to their living quarters in the White House.

President Bush, who retired in Houston following his re-election loss, will be remembered for the many times he accompanied or hosted astronauts while he served as the U.S. Ambassador to the United Nations in New York, his two terms as vice president to Ronald Reagan, and his one term as the U.S. President.

It was mid-afternoon when we departed the White House and arrived at National Airport, where our jet was waiting, and we were airborne by mid afternoon for the flight to Ellington Air Force Base near Houston.

The Apollo 11 astronauts participated in a series of workshops at the Johnson Space Center on Friday the 21, which featured many of the current and former astronauts. That night the crew was honored at a large civic dinner in downtown Houston, marking the end of the 20th anniversary.

With the conclusion of the anniversary activities, I began to reflect on my involvement with so many astronauts and historic events beginning with Apollo 8 in 1968. Astronauts from returning missions were honored guests at the two Richard Nixon inaugurations (1969 and 1973), ticker tape parades in New York and Chicago, a White House state dinner in Los Angeles, five Apollo astronaut crews made trips abroad on behalf of the U.S. President, countless visits to more than a hundred countries, every U.S. state and territories, audiences with the Pope, Paul VI, Queen Elizabeth and other Royalty and numerous heads of state.

Astronaut crews were honored at four NFL Super Bowls; Apollo 8 at Super Bowl III in Miami, Apollo 12, at Super Bowl IV in New Orleans, and Apollo 17 at Super Bowl VII in Los Angeles. Astronauts were also introduced and participated at the Rose, Fiesta, Orange and Sugar Bowls during the Apollo and Space Shuttle eras.

The NFL, wanting to recognize NASA following the tragic *Challenger* accident in 1986, featured a pre-game tribute before Super Bowl XXIII on January 22, 1989, in Miami. It featured introduction of astronauts representing the Mercury, Gemini and Apollo programs and all the members of the Space Shuttle *Atlantis* crew who completed a four day mission in December, the second successful shuttle flight after the *Challenger* disaster.

The program began with introduction of Mercury Astronaut Gordon Cooper, followed by Gemini and Apollo Astronauts Pete Conrad and Dick Gordon, and concluded with the introduction of the Space Shuttle (STS-27) *Atlantis* crew, Commander Robert (Hoot) Gibson, Guy Gardner, Richard Mullane, Jerry Ross and William Shepherd.

Following the tribute to NASA, a number of celebrities, including Gloria Estefan, Frankie Avalon, Annette Funicello, Billy Joel and Christie Brinkley were introduced and performed. Gibson and his crew surprised NFL Commissioner Pete Rozelle with an inscribed football that had traveled with them in space and had logged millions of miles.

It was a parting gift for the commissioner, who had announced his retirement earlier. The game was considered one of the best Super Bowls ever played, as San Francisco quarterback Joe Montana drove the 49ers on a game winning drive to beat the Cincinnati Bengals 20-16.

In looking back I realize how truly fortunate I was, to borrow from an old expression, to "have been in the right place at the right time" and to have been a part of the most exciting and challenging time in our country's history.

The opportunity to have worked and developed so many professional, and in many cases personal and lasting friendships is something for which I am truly grateful and blessed. Those with Neil Armstrong and Gene Cernan rank at the very top.

I am also fortunate to have worked with Michael Collins, Jim Lovell, Fred Haise, David Scott, Al Worden, Tom Stafford and Jack Schmitt. Some of my most memorable friendships include those made with many who are longer with us, including Pete Conrad, Dick Gordon, Alan Bean, Jack Swigert, Alan Shepard, Deke Slayton, Ron Evans and John Young, who deservedly earned the reputation as the most experienced man in space. I know there are many others that should be recognized, and my sincere apologies for failing to mention them here.

I was truly saddened when I learned that Neil had died unexpectedly at the age of 82 on August 25, 2012, following heart surgery complications. I had known Neil since 1969, and while he had left NASA in 1971, he never hesitated to call or stop by to discuss a public affairs matter. He valued my opinion, while not always agreeing with me. I felt honored to have earned his trust and confidence knowing that our conversations would remain confidential.

During the time he was on the University of Cincinnati faculty, he and his wife Janet operated an active farm outside the city of Lebanon. He also maintained a private office there where Miss Vivian White handled his correspondence and phone calls.

He and Janet divorced after 38 years of marriage in 1994. I remember his two young sons Mark and Rick from the hometown welcome in 1969, and saw them as good looking young men with their mother Janet when we attended together an Apollo event in Pensacola, Florida, in 2012.

Neil always felt a life-long commitment and obligation to NASA dating back to his time at the Lewis (now John Glenn) Research Center at Cleveland, his career as a civilian test pilot flying the X-15 seven times at Edwards Air Force Base, to his selection as an astronaut in 1962.

Making his first space flight as commander of the Gemini 8, and as commander of the historic Apollo 11 mission, he never hesitated to serve when called upon, like when President Reagan named him as a member of the Rogers Commission investigating the *Challenger* accident.

Our friendship included the exchange of Christmas cards for many years, and my wife Peg recalls his warm embrace and inquiring about me at Washington National Airport, where he had just arrived and she had just left me at another departing gate.

In fact, two of her most prized possessions are photos of her with Neil in 1979 and with Cernan in 2011.

I had been retired about 17 years when I received an invitation in the mail from the U.S, Congress to attend the presentation of Congressional Gold Medals to John Glenn and the three Apollo 11 astronauts at a ceremony in the Rotunda of the U.S. Capitol on November 16, 2011.

While seated in a reserved section and waiting for the beginning of the ceremony, I was summoned back stage where I had a chance to pay my respects and talk briefly with Neil, Mike and Buzz before returning to my seat to listen to remarks by the Senate and House leadership, followed by words of thanks and acceptance by Glenn and Armstrong.

The program featured music by noted artist Nora Jones and included her rendition of "America the Beautiful."

The Congressional Gold Medal and the Presidential Medal of Freedom are the highest civilian awards in the U.S. Glenn and Armstrong are recipients of both, joining the Wright Brothers among others dating back to the American Revolution. For Armstrong, who was decorated by 17 countries, it was the last of the many awards he received during an illustrious career because he died unexpectedly the following year in 2012.

It was only fitting that Cernan would be chosen by the Armstrong family to deliver the eulogy at his public memorial service at the National Cathedral in Washington, D.C. on September 13, 2012. While open to the public, many of the Cathedral's 1,500 seats were occupied by the Armstrong family, John and Annie Glenn, Buzz Aldrin, Mike Collins and many members of the NASA community. U.S. Senator Bob Portman, of Ohio and a close personal friend of Neil's also spoke.

Cernan's remarks were truly eloquent. "Fate looked down on us when she chose Neil to be the first to venture to another world and to have the opportunity to look back from space at the beauty of our own, choking up at times, he continued, "no one, but no one, no one would have accepted the responsibility of his remarkable accomplishment with more dignity and more grace than Neil Armstrong. He embodied all that is good and all that is great about America."

Mike Collins, who flew with Neil and Buzz Aldrin on that historic flight, led the assembly in prayers, saying: "Creator of the universe, your domination extends through the immensity of space. Guide and guard those who seek to fathom its mysteries.

"Especially, we thank you for this day for your servant Neil Armstrong, who with courage and humility first set foot upon the moon. Following his example, save us from the arrogance, lest we forget that our achievements are grounded in you."

While entitled to interment at Arlington National Cemetery, it was Neil's wish to be buried at sea. His cremated remains, accompanied by family, were carried aboard the USS *Philippine Sea* for the sea service burial off the Florida coast in the Atlantic Ocean on September 14.

Upon my retirement from NASA in 1994, my staff presented me with a number of letters from former and current astronauts thanking me for my service to them and extending best wishes for the future. I was most appreciative of all the letters, but the one I received from Neil was especially thoughtful and meaningful.

Three months after his death, Peg and I attended a Salute to the Pioneers of Space event at the Naval Aviation Museum in Pensacola, on

Saturday, December 15. We joined an impressive group of more than 1,200 that included many former astronauts, NASA officials, flight directors, engineers, scientists and others who had contributed to the success in the space race.

The night before, we attended a private anniversary reception and dinner hosted by Cernan, which featured the unveiling an Apollo Lunar Module exhibit to mark the 40th anniversary of his Apollo 17 mission.

Saturday's program began with Apollo 13 commander Jim Lovell and lunar module pilot Fred Haise, joined by flight controllers Gene Kranz, Gerry Griffin and Glynn Lunney, in a panel discussion describing the teamwork between the crew and Mission Control in bringing home the damaged spacecraft and saving the lives of the crew.

A luncheon followed and featured speeches by Glenn and Cernan. A reception and a "Salute to the Pioneers of Space" dinner that night included a performance by the "Up With People" vocal group and a special video tribute to Armstrong. There for the tribute were Janet Armstrong and sons Rick and Mark.

As the program ended, each guest departed with an impressive framed commemorative montage featuring a selection of iconic photographs and Apollo crew mission patches. Cernan's executive assistant, Claire Johnson, was credited with overseeing the many details for the events that left everyone there with a deeper appreciation for the sacrifices of the dedicated men and women being recognized and honored that weekend.

Chapter Seventeen

50TH ANNIVERSARY OF THE FIRST LUNAR LANDING

As we prepare to celebrate the 50th anniversary of the first lunar landing mission, let's remember that thirty-two astronauts had been assigned to fly in the Apollo program. Twenty-four of them left Earth's orbit and flew around the Moon on nine missions. Twelve walked on the Moon and six drove the Lunar Roving Vehicle. Three flew to the Moon twice and two landed (Young and Cernan) and none landed more than once.

Nine astronauts flew Apollo spacecraft during three Skylab missions, and Stafford commanded ASTP in an Apollo spacecraft. Hopefully the four surviving Moonwalkers—Aldrin, Scott, Duke and Schmitt—will be still be among us to celebrate that great achievement in 2019.

While I have so many memorable experiences with both Armstrong and Cernan, I would like to share one that occurred with Cernan in 1974.

He had left the astronaut corps that year to become program manager for the joint U.S. Soviet Apollo/Soyuz mission in 1975. His work involved making many trips to the Soviet Union to work with Russian counterparts as the senior NASA negotiator.

The U.S. Information Agency (USIA), aware that Cernan was making frequent trips to the Soviet Union, expressed interest in scheduling him for a series of appearances at their expense to then Yugoslavia, Czechoslovakia, and Romania.

He willingly agreed to the invitation, and especially the opportunity to appear in Czechoslovakia, the country of his family. I worked out the details with USIA and was assigned to staff the trip.

We rendezvoused in Vienna, where we spent the night at the home of the U.S. Ambassador before beginning our travels by train the following day. I had arrived with a suitcase of presentation items and photographs.

A USIA representative met us at each stop and accompanied us to a series of arranged events. Our first encounter with diplomatic protocol occurred on the train ride crossing the border into Czechoslovakia, when a burly border guard boarded the train and confronted us in a gruff manner with "Passports."

We presented our passports, and Cernan with pen in hand autographed an 8x10 lithograph of himself in the Apollo spacesuit. The guard was aghast and while they carried on a conversation about the significance of the autographed photo, I was able to leave the train and cross the tracks to the depot where I purchased ham and cheese sandwiches and a couple of beers.

Cernan had anticipated the visit to Czechoslovakia but he became very dismayed on our arrival in Prague, where he observed the influence of the Soviet Union who had crushed the country's bid for freedom in 1968. The Soviet presence was evident wherever we traveled, and the Soviets and local police seemed to monitor our every move.

Our U.S. embassy escort, who also was of Czech/American extraction, shared his displeasure with the Soviet influence in the country and arranged a clandestine meeting for Gene to meet secretly with a group of dissidents, who talked freely but were obviously concerned of being discovered. He expressed his personal feelings and distrust of the Soviets, and encouraged them to continue their fight for freedom.

He was especially upset during our visit to the Municipal House in Prague where the Royal Court was once located, which witnessed the proclamation of independent Czechoslovakia in 1918. Here in this national heritage building was the display of the Czech flag alongside the hammer and cycle of the Soviet Union.

Before our departure for Bucharest, Romania, Cernan asked if it would be possible to visit the family ancestral home called Vysoká nad, about two miles south of the Polish border. A helicopter flew him to the site while I remained behind.

On arrival he was met by the local commissar, whose welcoming remarks included a reference that Cernan related to me: "Your family would never have had to leave here today because things are now so much better."

Our final stop in Romania's Capital Bucharest featured Cernan's meeting with Elena Ceausescu, wife of the country's brutal dictator

Nicolae. He was out the country, but she was the country's deputy prime minister and known for her interest in science.

Cernan presented her with a flown Romanian flag and mission patch. Fifteen years later, the despised couple was overthrown in a violent revolution. They were caught fleeing and executed by a firing squad on Christmas Day 1989.

During the long flight back to the U.S. we had a chance to talk about our backgrounds, which were very similar. He was born a year earlier than me in 1934; both second generation Americans, he of Czech/Slovak descent and shared the same middle names Eugene, of our paternal grandfathers—he Andrew and me Arthur.

He retired from NASA and the U.S. Navy in July 1976, starting his own company, and later served as a co-anchorman on ABC-TV's coverage of the Space Shuttle program. In 1998 he published his autobiography, "Last Man on the Moon", which he used as the basis for a documentary film of the same name in 2014.

Over the years we kept in touch and occasionally managed to grab dinner and drinks at Cocoa Beach. We were very close to Gene and his first wife Barbara, and were disappointed when we learned of their divorce. Both remarried, but they remained close and shared in the raising of a beautiful daughter Tracy,

In early 2016, we received a personal handwritten note from Gene expressing his sympathy after learning of the death of our son Mick, a United Launch Alliance engineer in Florida in August of 2015. It was in the note that he extended a personal invitation to attend the world premiere showing of the documentary film" Last Man on the Moon" in Washington that February 26, which just happened to be on Peg's birthday.

Of course we attended and were able to spend some time talking to Gene and his former wife Barbara, who was there to participate in the premiere. When the program ended and we were preparing to leave. Gene sought us out again and expressed his emotional feelings over the loss of our son. It would be the last time we saw Gene because of his unexpected death on January 16, 2017.

We hadn't realized he had been hospitalized until we watched him interviewed on Fox News following the death of John Glenn. Gene was in a hospital gown, and it was obvious that he was in failing health.

We made immediate plans for a flight to Houston for the Visitation at the funeral home on Monday, January 23. His casket was adorned by an American flag, and I said my final goodbye by placing one hand on the casket and the other over my heart. Tracy had done a remarkable job of displaying hundreds of photographs and memorabilia of her father's life.

While it was a sad occasion, we were able to see and talk to many old friends from NASA, including astronauts Tom Stafford, Dave Scott, Jim and Marilyn Lovell, Walt Cunningham, Bill and Valerie Anders, flight directors Gerry Griffin and Glynn Lunney.

We were especially happy to see Claire Johnson, who Gene described as a petite Tennessee dynamo he hired forty-years earlier as a secretary who eventually became his executive assistant. It was there we learned from friends that Gene had been ill for several months, and many felt that his extensive travel here and abroad to promote the documentary contributed to his failing health. Knowing Gene, he wouldn't have had it any other way.

The funeral services were held the following day at St. Martin's Episcopal Church in Houston. It was beautifully planned and speaking as one who knew Cernan, it was as if he had done it himself. Everything about it bore his signature, and in effect it had when you realize Tracy had carried out the wishes of her father even before he left us.

The hour and a half service included a combination of religious readings, patriotism, and the personal eulogies by Fox News commentator Neil Cavuto, Lovell and retired U.S. Navy Commander Fred (Baldy) Baldwin, Cernan's longtime best friend who had begun their Navy careers together

The Reverend Dr. Russell J. Levenson, Jr. delivered an eloquent and moving tribute. He and Crernan had developed a unique friendship during his many days in the hospital, and they shared so much about life, religion and family. After his presentation, it was easy to understand why he had been selected by Gene to deliver his eulogy.

His name resurfaced with the death of Barbara Bush when we learned that she and President Bush were also St. Martin parishioners, and that he had been at her bedside praying with the family in her final moments and would be the celebrant at her funeral services on April 21, 2018.

Cernan's burial services were held at the Texas State Cemetery, near Austin. It was again an opportunity to see and visit with many old friends, including Charles (Charlie) Bolden, the former astronaut who just days earlier had resigned as the NASA Administrator after eight years. He was there to pay his respects to someone he had come to know and respect.

Dr. Levenson presided over the military funeral services on Wednesday, January 25, which included a flyover of vintage Navy aircraft. I will always remember and be grateful for having got to know, love and admire a true American hero.

His burial site, which he himself selected, sits high on a hill where he has a beautiful view not far from his ranch in Kerrville, a retreat where he loved to ride his horses and work with his longhorn cows and fish and hunt.

About a year before he retired from the Navy and left NASA, Cernan presented me with a flown miniature U.S. Flag and a note typed on NASA letterhead dated December 7, 1975 and two small pieces of the outer skin of the Command Module *America* removed after the historic flight and encased in Lucite.

The first and last men to walk on the Moon had so much in common. Both were University of Purdue graduates, former U.S. Naval aviators, test pilots and becoming astronauts a year apart, Armstrong in 1962 and Cernan in 1963. While they occupy a special place in space flight history, things could have changed if each had not survived earlier crashes in training flight vehicles.

A year before the first lunar landing, Armstrong ejected safely just moments before the crash of his Lunar Landing Training Vehicle (LLTV) at Ellington Air Force Base. Cernan was flying a Bell 476 helicopter out of Patrick Air Force Base in Florida on January 23, 1971, when at about 300 feet the craft lost altitude and crashed. Cernan survived and was able to swim away as the chopper's fuel tank exploded and a fire quickly spread.

He suffered minor burns and was assisted by a 19-year-old boy in a nearby boat. While it was feared that the accident could jeopardize his assignment as the Apollo 17 commander, NASA determined the crash was not the result of human error and he continued on to earn his place in history.

The distinction of being the last person to walk on the moon was an honor he always held dear, but was certain it would eventually belong to someone else. His biggest disappointment was this country's failure to continue the manned space effort back to the Moon, Mars and beyond.

Armstrong and Cernan are the bookends to man's presence on the Moon—from Armstrong's "One giant leap for mankind" as the first human to step on the lunar surface on July 20, 1969, to Cernan's "As we leave the Moon at Taurus-Littrow, we leave as we came and, God willing, as we shall return: with peace and hope for all mankind" on December 14, 1972.

Neither capitalized on their celebrity status, but instead wanted to be remembered as team players whose contributions along with those of thousands of others, remains the "Golden Age of NASA" after 50 years. There is no way to describe the mutual respect and admiration each had for the other.

ABOUT THE AUTHOR

Gene Marianetti was born in 1935, the only child of Gino and Minnie (Grasseschi), both first generation Italian-Americans whose parents had immigrated from northern Italy and settled in Black Eagle, a small community of mostly Italian and Croatian immigrants near Great Falls, Montana, on the Missouri River.

He was born as the country was emerging from the Great Depression, spent his grade school years as the country was fighting World War II, and began high school at the start of the Korean War in 1950.

After high school in 1954, he enrolled at the University of Montana in Missoula where he majored in Journalism. Midway through his freshman year he decided to pursue a radio broadcasting career and enrolled at the Brown Institute of the Air in Minneapolis, Minnesota.

He and his high school sweetheart Peggy Hasbrouck married after her graduation and they moved to Minneapolis for the beginning of the school year. A son Randy was born while there.

Following graduation, Gene was hired by KBTK, a small radio station in Missoula at a starting salary of $.75 cents an hour, the minimum wage at the time, while Peg helped supplement their income with a job at a local bank, after giving birth to a second son Michael in 1957.

KBTK employed a small staff of announcers who like him, worked full time while attending classes at the university. The time at Brown's had prepared him for a variety of on the air experiences, including the gathering, preparing and reading local news.

As he gained experience he received an offer in 1959 from radio station KMON in Great Falls to become its first full time news director, which included a significant pay raise. In a six-year career there he received nine broadcasting excellence awards from the Associated Press.

In 1965 he decided on a career change and applied for a year's internship offered by Montana's junior U.S. Senator Lee Metcalf, to serve on the Senator's staff in his Washington, D.C. office beginning in September. He was one of 32 applicants for the job when he received word of his selection. The family now numbered five with the birth of daughter Jamie Lynn in 1960.

As a member of the Senator's staff, he wrote a weekly newsletter and produced a TV interview show for distribution to TV stations in Montana, and the prime responsibility of producing TV and radio commercials for use in the Senator's first re-election campaign in 1966. Metcalf defeated the incumbent Republican Governor (Tim Babcock) by 12,000 votes.

As the internship was nearing its end, Gene began exploring positions in the U.S. Government. His broadcast career and the year on the Senator's staff earned him several interviews, including the one that resulted in a position with the National Aeronautics and Space Administration (NASA) Headquarters in Washington in 1967.

In August of that year, he became a protocol officer in the office of public affairs, responsible for the astronaut public appearances program and later his job was expanded to include development of an agency-wide program for the invitation and accommodation of guests and the general public for the upcoming Apollo program scheduled to begin in 1968. At the time NASA was recovering from the Apollo 1 fire, which resulted in the deaths of three astronauts.

A fourth and final child, Kelly Thresa was born on election night in November of that year, about the time that Richard M. Nixon had been declared the 37th President-Elect of the U.S.

Gene's NASA career spanned 27 years and he was involved with some of the most historic and iconic events and individuals during NASA's Golden Years.

His work was recognized with the award of three NASA Exceptional Service Awards in 1973, 1981 and 1990. The award is second only to the NASA Distinguished Service Award.

He was most proud however, when he received the "Silver Snoopy" personal achievement award from Astronaut Rick Hauck in 1989. The award is recognition of an individual's work and dedication to the astronauts, and features an image of cartoon character Snoopy in the Peanuts series and was approved for use in the NASA Manned Flight Awareness Program by creator and cartoonist Charles Schultz.

He retired in 1994 to Locust Grove, Virginia about halfway between Washington and Richmond. He enjoys golf and driving a restored 1957 Ford Thunderbird and spending time with three surviving children and four great grand children.

Index

ALSO BY
ACCLAIM PRESS

The Greatest Space Generation
Edited by Ed Buckbee
6x9, 320 pages, hardcover • 978-1-942613-22-0• $29.95

The Greatest Space Generation is the story of the scientists, engineers, managers, and skilled workers who created the Saturn rocket—a magnificent space machine—to take American astronauts to the Moon. It's about those who came to Huntsville, Alabama, because of the work underway at Redstone Arsenal and later, Marshall Space Flight Center. They were the trailblazers for both missile defense and peaceful exploration of outer space.

These pages reveal what it was like to be a rocket scientist working on cutting edge technology in space sciences, guidance and control, fabrication and quality control. It took German vision plus American initiative to beat the Russians to the Moon. The Moon landing, widely acknowledged as the single most important technological achievement in the 20th century, launched a new economy in Huntsville.

Manned spaceflight will always be a testament to mankind's capacity to imagine, create, explore and grow. The Moon was the first, but far from the final, destination. Will there ever be a generation to match the speed, courage and passion of the Apollo days? Only time will tell, but without a doubt, America will stand on the shoulders of the Greatest Space Generation to step foot on Mars and beyond.

The Real Space Cowboys
Ed Buckbee
6x9, 256 pages, hardcover • 978-1-942613-77-0 • $29.95

The Real Space Cowboys tells the story of America's Mercury 7 astronauts, who volunteered to be the first to explore the unknown perils of spaceflight beginning in the late 1950s.

Detailed interviews with the Mercury 7—Alan Shepard, Gus Grissom, John Glenn, Scott Carpenter, Wally Schirra, Gordon Cooper, and Deke Slayton—provide a first-hand account of the competition, controversies, training, and hard work that took them a step beyond their former lives as cocky military pilots.

The book also tells the story of the twelve brave Moonwalkers who actually landed on the Moon, Wernher von Braun and his team of rocket scientists who developed the technology to propel men and materials into space, the Russian Cosmonauts and Chinese Taikonauts who helped fuel the competitive space race, plus humorous stories of the pranks and goofs the Mercury 7 enjoyed to pull on each other.

Written by Ed Buckbee, a public affairs officer under Wernher von Braun who founded U.S. Space Camp and was personal friends with the Mercury 7, The Real Space Cowboys is a fitting tribute to the origins of manned space flight and the men who blazed that trail into the unknown.

With the 50th Anniversary of the first Moon landing scheduled for July 20, 2019, now is the perfect time to reflect on these great pilots as future pioneers plan new adventures in space flight.

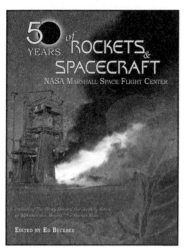

50 Years of Rockets & Spacecraft: NASA Marshall Space Center

Ed Buckbee
9x12, 224 pages, hardcover • 978-1-935001-17-1 • $44.95

U.S. manned space flight began in the Rocket City, Huntsville, Alabama. It's the home of the George C. Marshall Space Flight Center, America's premier rocket center.

The men and women, who made up the Marshall team, tell their story in *50 Years of Rockets and Spacecraft*. It's an exciting space history lesson beginning with Alan Shepard's flight on the Mercury-Redstone and continuing with Saturn rocket rides to the moon, Skylab, Space Shuttle, International Space Station, Hubble, Ares and the future.

Wernher von Braun's personal Weekly Notes, recently discovered in the archives, are published and reviewed for the first time. One can feel the passion, the dedication and commitment that team members demonstrated on a daily basis following what von Braun often referred to as the "critical path" to the moon.

The book contains personal behind the scenes stories told by the men and woman who made critical decisions to send American astronauts on journeys into space and on to the moon. The stories range from humorous anecdotes to gut-wrenching decisions required to safely fly humans to this new frontier.

50 Years of Rockets and Spacecraft is the Marshall team's story – first-person account – of the dramatic and historic space flight accomplishments that have taken place at America's premier rocket center.

Smoke Jumper, Moon Pilot: The Remarkable Life of Apollo 14 Astronaut Stuart Roosa

Willie G. Moseley
6x9, 256 pages, hardcover • 978-1-935001-76-8 • $24.95

Stu Roosa's life was incredibly diverse—the second son of a government surveyor, he had spent his early childhood in a migratory lifestyle with his family before the Roosas settled in Claremore, Oklahoma.

He became a smoke jumper for the Forest Service before enlisting in the Air Force's aviation cadet program. Excelling in piloting skills, Roosa had graduated from test pilot school at the legendary Edwards Air Force Base before being chosen as an astronaut.

Roosa loved his family and his country, and he loved to fly. Recollections in this detailed biography include memories from family members, schoolmates, and veteran smoke jumpers, pilots, and astronauts.

Smoke Jumper, Moon Pilot tells the story of a focused, determined, and patriotic youngster who believed in the American dream, and grew up to live it.